Life and Teaching of Two Immortals

Volume II: Chen Tuan

The Teaching of the Integral Way

as presented by Hua-Ching Ni

T   *stands for Truth*

A   *stands for Above*

O   *stands for Oneself*

Thus, Tao stands for
TRUTH ABOVE ONESELF.

Also,

T   *stands for Truth*

A   *stands for Among*

O   *stands for Ourselves*

Thus, at the same time, Tao stands for
TRUTH AMONG OURSELVES.

Life and Teaching of Two Immortals

Volume II: Chen Tuan

By NI, HUA-CHING
Teacher of Natural Spiritual Truth

SevenStar Communications
SANTA MONICA

Acknowledgement: Thanks and appreciation to Suta Cahill, Janet DeCourtney and the mentors in Atlanta for typing, editing and desktop publishing this book.

SevenStar Communications
an imprint of Sevenstar Communications Group, Inc.
1314 Second Street #208
Santa Monica, California 90401

The paper used in this publication meets the minimum requirements of the American National Standard for Information Sciences Permanence of Paper for Printed Library Materials, ANSI 239.48-1984.

First Printing February 1993

Library of Congress Cataloging In Publication Data

Ni, Hua Ching.
   Life and teaching of two immortals.

   Includes index.
   Contents: v. 1. Kou Hong -- v. 2. Chen Tuan.
   1. Spiritual life--Taoism. I. Ko, Hung, 284-364.
II. Ch'en, T'uan, ca. 885-989. III. Title.
BL1923.N538 1992   299'.514448   91-62058
ISBN 0-937064-47-5 (pkb. : v.1)
ISBN 0-937064-48-3 (v. 2)

This book is dedicated
to those who pursue the subtle reality of life
which is not confined or limited
by the physical form of life.

To female readers,

According to natural spiritual teaching, male and female are equally important in the natural sphere. This is seen in the diagram of Tai Chi. Thus, discrimination is not practiced in our tradition. All my work is dedicated to both genders of human people.

Wherever possible, constructions using masculine pronouns to represent both sexes are avoided; where they occur, we ask your tolerance and spiritual understanding. We hope that you will take the essence of my teaching and overlook the superficiality of language. Gender discrimination is inherent in English; ancient Chinese pronouns do not have differences of gender. I wish that all of you achieve above the level of language or gender.

Thank you, H. C. Ni

Warning - Disclaimer

This book presents information and techniques that have been in use throughout the orient for many years. These practices utilize a natural system within the body; however, there are no claims for effectiveness. The information offered is to the author's best knowledge and experience and is to be used by the reader(s) at their own discretion and liability. It can be beneficial or harmful depending upon one's stage of development.

Because of the sophisticated nature of the information contained within this book, it is recommended that the reader also study the author's other books for further understanding of a healthy lifestyle and energy-conducting exercises. You need to accept legal responsibility for doing a thing you do not thoroughly understand.

Because people's lives have different conditions and different stages of growth, no rigid or strict practice can be applied universally. Thus, it must be through the discernment of the reader that the practices are selected. The adoption and application of the material offered in this book is totally your own responsibility.

The author and publisher of this book are not responsible in any manner for any injury that may occur through following the instructions in this book.

Contents

Master Chen Tuan

Prelude

The Subtle Essence conveyed by the teaching of the Integral Way is the deep truth of all religions, yet it transcends all religions, leaving them behind as clothing worn in different seasons or places. The teaching of the Subtle Essence includes everything of religious importance, yet it goes beyond the level of religion. It directly serves your life, surpassing the boundary of all religions and extracting the essence of them all.

The Subtle Essence as conveyed by the teaching of the Integral Way is also the goal of all sciences, but it surpasses all sciences, leaving them behind as partial and temporal descriptions of this universal Integral Truth. Unlike any partial science, the Way goes beyond the level of any single scientific search.

The Subtle Essence is the master teaching. It does not rely on any authority. It is like a master key which can unlock all doors directly leading you to the inner room of the ultimate truth. It is not frozen at the emotional surface of life. It does not remain locked at the level of thought or belief with the struggling which extends to skepticism and endless searching.

The teaching of the One Great Path of the Subtle Essence presents the core of the Integral Truth and helps you reach it yourself.

Preface

In spiritual learning, if your purpose is to look for spiritual development, it is important to know the right school. Otherwise, seriousness would cause you to misuse the opportunity of a lifetime as you applied yourself diligently to the wrong learning. The real teaching of the Subtle Truth has no rigidifying external style to choose from, like restaurants that offer different "cuisine." It teaches the true knowledge of food and cooking in order to give you real benefit, instead of only pleasing your palate. This is the fundamental difference. Lao Tzu said, the teaching of the Integral Way is like unspiced food; although it does not appeal to your taste buds, it is more nutritious. (Chapter 35 of the *Tao Teh Ching*.)

Also, the Subtle Essence is the spirituality of the universe and of mankind. It is too subtle to describe; you can only learn about it from the comparative study of the existing examples - the religions. In my work I frequently make use of them and comment about them to achieve this purpose. However, only a few classics such as those by Lao Tzu and Chuang Tzu discussed the Subtle Essence. In these two volumes, I make a new attempt.

In later times and later generations, the teaching of the Subtle Essence became blended with or was being used to support the establishment of religion. As a result, however, the teaching of spiritual truth was contorted and could not be maintained as the open and broad spiritual education for all people. Religions do not teach enlightenment; they teach different types of practices which have other purposes and functions.

Aside from following religions which are very easy to contact, you might be interested in doing your own spiritual development. Spiritual development is more important than political or social independence. You do not allow anybody else to manage your life, in things as small as your finances; why allow religions or anyone else to manage this essential part of your life spiritually?

In this two-volume set, I present two individuals who had spiritual interest and years of cultivation and achievement. They are the good model for spiritual students and teachers.

This book, *The Life and Teaching of Two Immortals*, has been divided into two volumes which present Master Kou Hong and Master Chen Tuan respectively. Master Kou Hong lived around 1,700 years ago, and Master Chen Tuan around 1,000 years ahead. They are both models of spiritual development that can serve to inspire us. About half of the material that each master taught was for enlightenment and wisdom. The other half comprised useful and effective spiritual practices which could bring about a result different than religions teach. These practices, when applied to a healthy life, can lead a person to complete development of himself or herself as a human individual. The lives of these two great teachers expressed that they were completely developed, balanced individuals.

Balance is an important part of a healthy personality. Each individual is born with self-nature; self-nature is the spiritual nature of people. This is the common reality of the existence of every person and thing in the universe, yet the approach to realize one's spiritual self-nature can take one of two main ways. One way of realizing oneself is to cultivate one's spirit in solitude. This way holds the belief that mingling with general society is akin to murdering one's own spiritual nature. This way leads to people leaving society and becoming hermits. In solitude, no self is displayed, which brings great spiritual enjoyment. The other way of realizing oneself is to cultivate one's spirit through social work or activity. This way leads to people becoming great leaders or helpers of society. In a group of people, one is constantly aware of the self. This brings the need of constant refinement and improvement.

Both Masters Kou Hong and Chen Tuan began their lives with strong spiritual interest. Both extended the range of their lives to include each of the two ways to spiritual achievement, spiritual enjoyment and worldly service. During their lives, they responded to what was needed in the world. Both were engaged in war. Kou Hong went to war to set an example of minimizing killing to restore the order in society. Chen Tuan was famous for his "sleeping." In his "sleep," he extended himself to the activity of restoring peace in a society stricken with military competition of the warlords. He provided people with a chance to rest, be safe and find a new life with better opportunity, and ended a 52-year span of turmoil in society.

After peace was restored, both Master Chen Tuan and Master Kou Hong taught in their own informal schools. Both directed their teachings for open spiritual achievement rather than promoting a rigid religion to pass themselves as leaders of society. Their model of life greatly impressed my young heart; thus, it was my choice to continue their teaching. I like to live a life of spiritual enjoyment away from all possible disturbances, but I also respond to the current world problems. I preserve and revive all truly beneficial teachings and achievements of different generations for people who need to stabilize their spiritual position to live in a new time, a new world of new thoughts and new confusion.

In the book of Master Kou Hong, there is one chapter of philosophical level material. Although it is not directly Kou Hong's teaching, it is also Kou Hong's spirit to offer guidance appropriate to all times and all places.

In the book of Master Chen Tuan, there are two chapters of philosophical material. Before Chen Tuan, or at the time of Chen Tuan, Chinese scholars focused on the pursuit of governmental positions to share ruling power over ordinary people. Master Chen Tuan's philosophical influence on Chinese scholars was to change their focus from seeking position and fame to searching for spiritual truth. Although the material in these two chapters was not written directly by him, it reflects Master Chen Tuan's philosophical orientation which helped the scholars to open up. New inspiration came to them when they studied the old inspiration of the Subtle Essence.

It brought great happiness to scholars and teachers in different generations to rediscover the Subtle Essence, which is related to their own eternal life. Although some of this material may be different from what you are used to, and hard to digest or understand all at once, I hope you have patience with it and read several lines, several paragraphs or several pages at one time. Reread these books or parts if necessary. I am sure you will be rewarded by your efforts, and hope that you will find these two books enjoyable and helpful.

Sincerely,
Your Spiritual Friend
Ni, Hua-Ching

Chapter 1

The Active Sleeping Sage

I

After the glory of the Tang Dynasty (618-906 A.D.) faded, there was much competition among the warlords to build a new dynasty. Nevertheless, there was one spiritual person who subtly guided ambitious young men to end the confusion and disorder of this warring time. This spiritually achieved one remained a hermit and stayed unattached to worldly glory without any interest in worldly position or possession. Even so, he also earned great respect as a scholar who attained special capabilities such as foreknowledge through his study of the *Book of Changes.*

Master Chen Tuan was a person who exercised his spiritual influence as a cultural and spiritual leader who eventually started a new epoch. There is no real need for me to talk about how greatly he influenced his time. I would like to talk about his personal story and his famous sleeping cultivation.

Master Chen Tuan said, "If anybody goes to bed, lies down and can fall asleep peacefully, this must be a happy person. If a person lies down restlessly on his pillow and can hardly fall asleep, the person's mind must be occupied with some trouble." He respected peaceful sleeping. This made many people think Master Chen Tuan spent a lot of time asleep. Legend has it that he once slept for 800 years. That could not be true because he only lived to be 118 years old, but he did spend a lot of time in sleeping meditation. He choose two different mountains in which to stay and sleep.

Master Chen Tuan had four opportunities to be noble and rich during his lifetime. During each of the four newly established dynasties, the new emperors offered him high governmental positions, but he refused all of them. It is not believed that he was ever married; he enjoyed his spiritual freedom. His sleep was not sleep as most people think of it; his sleep was a type of internal energy cultivation. As I see it, falling asleep was how he kept his privacy when he did not choose to respond to visitors. In that way, undeveloped people could not bother him.

Master Chen Tuan was born in Tsing-Yuan of Hanchow. When he was five or six years old, he was not very communicative, so people called him a dumb child. One day, when he was about nine years old, he played at the side of a lake, and a woman immortal wearing deep blue clothing took him to the mountain. He received a gift from that lady; a book. She also wrote him a poem which went like this:

> *The herb I gathered is not enough to fill the basket,*
> *so I am going further up in the high mountains.*
> *I will point out where you need to go*
> *to return to your life.*
> *Some day, you will be the companion*
> *of the boundless green mountains.*

After being with her, Chen Tuan had a powerful understanding, because his mind had opened up. He came back home and recited the poem, which startled his father and mother. "Who taught you that?" they asked him. Chen Tuan told his parents what happened and showed them the book. It was the *Book of Changes.* He studied and learned it. After he had worked with that book, he could understand all other important spiritual books, but he only kept a few spiritual books for personal use. One was the *Book of Changes,* the other was the sacred book of Hwang Ting called *The Secret of Yellow Altar* and the third was Lao Tzu's *Tao Teh Ching.* By studying them, it seemed that he gave up what ordinary scholars pursue, which is a position with the government.

When Chen Tuan was 18 years old, his father and mother passed away. He gave up all the inheritance from his parents by distributing it to all the folks in the village. He only took one simple cooking tool with him and went to live in a nearby mountain. On the mountain, the immortal lady came to him in spirit. She taught him how to refine his bodily energy to be chi, chi to be sen, and sen to be nothing, which can be controlled. He followed and practiced this on the mountain. His footprints were never to appear in towns or cities.

At that time, many scholars admired and respected him as a living immortal. They wished to see him and learn from him, but people had trouble locating him. Some people went to a lot of trouble to find him only to discover that he was sleeping. Thus, he gave them no response. Most people had no patience to wait for him and would just go away.

At the end of the Rear Tang Dynasty (923-935 A.D.), Emperor Ming Tzung (reign 926-934 A.D.) heard about Master Chen Tuan and wrote a letter to him. He sent an officer to invite Master Chen Tuan to the royal court. One after another, the Emperor's messengers went to the mountain to persuade Master Chen Tuan to go see the emperor. He had no way to excuse himself - at that time the power of the sovereign was absolute and people had to do whatever he wanted - so Chen Tuan followed one messenger to Lo Yang, the capital. When he saw the Emperor, however, he just gave an ordinary bow. He was not like all the people who kneel down seriously before the Emperor to beg favor. All the officials and ministers were startled and astonished by his seeming lack of respect for their sovereign.

The Emperor himself did not feel upset by this lack of politeness. He gave Master Chen Tuan a beautiful cushion and asked him to sit at his side. The Emperor said, "It is precious for you to come so long a way to see me and give me the opportunity to see your pure light. It is the blessing of my three lifetimes."

The Emperor continued, "Since you are here, I have some really important matters to discuss with you, and I wish your advice." However, before the Emperor could speak further, Chen Tuan was sound asleep and gave no response. The Emperor used many different ways to try to make Chen Tuan work for him and give him advice.

During that time, the weather was cold and rainy, Chen Tuan was given a special room in the palace in which to rest. He only sat in meditation and slept in cultivation, and did nothing else. The Emperor took the advice of one of his ministers and chose three young and beautiful women with lovely clothes and sent them to him with good food and wine. The young women went to him and said, "We have come to warm your feet. Please don't refuse." Master Chen Tuan opened the wine and drank it. He also did not refuse the women. On the second day, when the Emperor came to see him, he found that the three women were locked in an empty room; Master Chen Tuan had disappeared. The Emperor asked the women where Master Chen Tuan went. They replied, "After drinking the wine and sleeping on the mattress, he said, 'Thank you for coming. I do not have anything to give you, so I will write a poem for you.' He gave us the poem but then he put us in this room and locked it, so we do not know where he went." Then the women gave the poem to the Emperor. The poem read,

> *Their bodies are made from snow,*
> *Their faces are made from jade.*
> *Thank you, our Emperor,*
>   *for sending them to me.*
> *I do not have that sweet dream with women,*
>   *so the coming of those beauties was in vain.*

After reading the poem, the Emperor understood that there was no way that he could make Chen Tuan work for him.

This time, when Chen Tuan left the Emperor, he chose a new place to go. He selected another mountain called Wu Dang mountain, a beautiful place with 27 high peaks, 36 big boulders and 24 creeks. In ancient times, this mountain was a place where a spiritual immortal could achieve himself.

II

One day, five old men came to visit Master Chen Tuan to discuss the meaning of *The Book of Changes* and the eight trigrams. Chen Tuan explained them and answered in detail. When Chen Tuan carefully observed the old men, he saw that their faces looked very fresh. He asked them, "What is the way to cultivate oneself?" The five old men told him about the way of human energy preservation. This type of vitality preservation is similar to the hibernation of the snake or turtle. Snakes and turtles hibernate and do not eat during the whole cold season. They told him the following story as an illustration.

Once there was a person who had a bed which was rotting; the legs were uneven and he needed to prop one of them up, so he used a turtle to support the rotten foot of the bed. After twenty years, he moved the bed and discovered that the turtle was still alive. It was proof that energy could be maintained for a long period of time. Master Chen Tuan also learned how to stop eating so that sometimes one period of sleep or hibernation could last for several months. Without learning this, a person would wake up when his stomach made some noise inside.

Master Chen Tuan lived on Wu Dang Mountain for over twenty years. At that time, he was already in his seventies. One day, the five old men came to see him again. They said, "We are the five dragons (spiritual energy beings) from the ponds of sun and moon (the solar system). This is not your place any longer; it has no more benefit for you. We received your instruction, your teaching on the *Book of Changes*, now we would like to help take you to a better place." Then they asked Master Chen Tuan to close his eyes. When he opened his eyes, after only a split second, he did not see five people any more, but discovered that he was on top of Hua Mountain, a big mountain thousands of miles to the west of Wu Dang Mountain. Master Chen Tuan decided to stay there. Many spiritual people had lived on that mountain before him, as well as while he was there, and also after he made the mountain famous. Many new people came along to stay on the mountain because they wished to learn from him. They wondered how he could live without any provisions or a kitchen; it seemed unusual. They quietly observed him and soon discovered that he did not do anything but sleep.

One day, Chen Tuan left the place where he was staying on Hua Mountain, which was called Nan Boulder. He did not return, so the other people living on the mountain who were cultivating themselves suspected that he had gone to another place. However, one day much later, when they went to the place where they had piled up the firewood, they discovered that he was sleeping back there! Because he went to sleep there when the firewood was plentiful and piled high, he had been able to sleep for a long time without being noticed by anyone. Only when the firewood had almost all been used did they discover him sleeping there.

Another time, a wood cutter discovered a corpse lying by the roadside. The wood cutter took pity on the corpse, and wished to dig a hole to bury it. However, when he came close to it, he discovered that it was the renowned Master Chen Tuan. The woodcutter said, "How can you die here?" At that moment, Master Chen Tuan stretched and opened his eyes, saying, "I was sleeping so nicely; why did you disturb me?" The woodcutter laughed. Master Chen Tuan knew the places with good energy that could support his cultivation.

Shortly after that, the magistrate of Hua Yin County traveled to Hua mountain to interview Chen Tuan. When he arrived at the mountain, he only saw a bare mountain covered with boulders; there was no house at all. He asked Chen Tuan, "Where do you stay?" Chen Tuan laughed and answered him with a poem. He said,

The high grassy mountain is my palace.
When I am out, I ride the wind.
I do not need to guard or lock my home.
It always has clouds to seal up the entrance,
    so people do not approach.

The magistrate wished to build a hut or temple for him. Chen Tuan did not accept. This was around 954-960 A. D.

The magistrate reported his experience to the new Emperor. During that period of history, there were many emperors, one after another. The Emperor knew that Master Chen Tuan was a spiritually achieved person and wished that Chen tuan would tell him how long his dynasty would last, so he sent a messenger to the mountain to look for him. Chen Tuan responded to his question with a poem of four lines:

A good tree is lush and strong
    and grows where there is no competition.
If you wish to keep it long,
    it is suitable to put a canopy over the tree.

The Emperor's surname was Firewood, so he interpreted the poem as complimenting his name and promising him a long reign. He really thought the poem was a nice way to praise him, but he did not know that it was the prophecy of a new dynasty coming after his reign. Chen Tuan was saying that his reign needed to be protected or be free from competition in order to be successful. The Emperor fell shortly after, and the Sung Dynasty (960-1279 A.D.), began.

That Emperor, whose name was Firewood, Emperor Szi Tzung (reign 954-960 A.D.) wished to offer a high position to

Chen Tuan, who insisted on staying in the mountain. At this time, the Emperor gave him a title derived from a line in one of Chen Tuan's poems. The Emperor called him "Master White Clouds."

III

Some years later, there was a rebellion at a place called Chen Bridge by some soldiers who disliked the government. General Jao was supported by the soldiers who declared their allegiance to him if he became the new Emperor. On that day, Master Chen Tuan rode his donkey to the city of Hua Yin. When he heard about this rebellion, he expressed his joy. People asked him, "Why should you be happy?" Master Chen Tuan told the people, "This is the new dynasty that will last and bring peace to the people." How did he know that? Many years previous, when the northern tribe started a military invasion into central China, all the people fled for safety, Master Chen Tuan among them. As he walked on the road, he saw a woman balancing a pole on her shoulders with a basket on each end of the pole. In each basket was a baby boy. When Master Chen Tuan saw the boys, he immediately knew that they would become the future leaders of the society. His prophecy was "People wonder who will be the lord of peace of China. The two Emperors sit in the baskets." Years later, the boys became the first and second Emperor of the Sung Dynasty (960-1279 A.D.) The woman was their mother, the future Queen Mother. He saw these small babies about 25 years before they actually took the throne.

Once many years after seeing the baby boys, Master Chen Tuan was touring Charng An City. Master Chen Tuan went into an inn and saw them there, but of course the baby boys were already grown up. They all sat together with a friend in a small inn and enjoyed drinking. Master Chen Tuan knew that their friend would become the future premier and he hinted to the man, "You shall be a star shining next to the big star." The elder of the two brothers overheard the remark and asked, "Who is this old gentleman?" Someone answered, "This is the famous Master White Clouds." The young man requested of him, "What is my future?" Master Chen Tuan replied, "Both you and your brother will be big shining stars in the sky." This gave lots of confidence to both young men and inspired their ambition to become Emperor and to benefit the people of the country through a peaceful reign. Later, they truly made an effort and exercised their talent and energy to end the time of confusion and bring peace to people. When they were on the throne, they sent an invitation many times to Master Chen Tuan to come and share the glory, but Master Chen Tuan responded by writing on the back of their invitation:

> You do not need to send a red phoenix
> to carry the invitation.
> My mind of wilderness only attaches
> to the white clouds.

It means he did not wish to go, but wanted to stay in the mountains. With this reply, the Emperor of the Sung dynasty let him be free.

After the first Emperor died, his brother took the throne. One day he recalled the prophecy that Master Chen Tuan had given them in the restaurant, and he wished to see him. The Emperor wrote a poem to invite him to come and see him. The poem said,

> You were honored as Master White Clouds
> by the previous dynasty,
> but you remained free and unknown to others.
> If now you would like to come to me,
> I will offer you a mountain with high peaks.

This time, Master Chen Tuan went to see the Emperor. The Emperor bade him sit down and asked him how a person should cultivate oneself. He was referring to the self-cultivation of a spiritually achieved person. Master Chen Tuan responded, "Your responsibility is to take care of the world. If you learn only how to cultivate yourself, you can ascend to Heaven on a bright day, but what benefit would that bring to all people? For a long time, people have not had a good life. If you have a clear mind and can choose capable and upright ministers, and if you can choose the right policies and the correct way to fulfill them, that is your spiritual cultivation. Anything beyond that is of a less spiritual nature."

The Emperor happily accepted and valued this advice, and asked, "What can I do for you?" Chen Tuan replied, "I have no desire, I would only like a place to enjoy my peace." So the Emperor allowed him to live on the mountain tax free and built a temple for him. Master Chen Tuan did not use the temple himself; he let his students use it. He himself still remained as a companion of the white clouds among the mountain peaks.

Some time later, he stayed somewhere in the countryside of the capital city. At that time, the Emperor wished to use military force to restore some territory beyond the northeast side of the Yellow River. He sent someone to ask Master Chen Tuan if he would win the battle. Master Chen Tuan wrote one word on the palm of the messenger, "Peace." When the Emperor saw that, he was unhappy about the result, but he had already started the military movement and could not stop. When he sent a message again to ask him for advice, Master Chen Tuan did not answer; he had gone to sleep. Every day the messenger wished to receive an answer from him, but for three months Master Chen Tuan did not get up, so there was no way to ask him. The battle did not succeed, and the soldiers and generals returned home in vain.

One day, Master Chen Tuan suddenly came into the royal palace and said, "Today I come to say farewell to you." The Emperor had wished to make him an advisor to whom he could frequently look for advice. In response, Master Chen Tuan gave a poem. It said,

> *Your majesty's searching for me*
> > *reached the wild rural place.*
> *I am a person who enjoys mountains of peace.*
> *When worldly things are always changing,*
> > *I keep my free life within the four oceans.*
> *I find joy from my own nature.*
> *I can befriend people by poem-writing.*
> *Please let me be what I am.*
> *Yet wherever I will be,*
> > *I am still in your service.*

> *P. S. After 2 years, I will come back to see you.*

The Emperor knew that Chen Tuan could not be kept, so he let him go back to the mountain and gave an order that no one could hunt where he stayed. The Emperor could give only one thing back to him: his freedom.

After the Emperor had been on the throne for 20 years, he could not decide which of his sons should take over the throne. On the ninth day of the ninth month, his eldest son became unhappy with his father and burned down his palace, so the Emperor was angry. The father loved his third son, but he was not sure that the son could handle the job of Emperor. Suddenly the Emperor recalled, Master Chen Tuan knows people, he even had the foreknowledge of himself, his brother and his friend. If Master Chen Tuan could come here now, how easy it would be to make the decision. Before his thought ended, the doorman came in to say, "Master Chen Tuan is here and wishes to see you."

The Emperor bid him enter and said, "What is the purpose of this visit?" Master Chen Tuan answered, "I have come to help you because you have doubt in your mind." The Emperor laughed and said, "We know you have true foreknowledge. My third son seems like a kind person and may have the capacity to be Emperor, but I really do not know whether or not he is the right person for this important position. I would like you to look at him and give me your advice." Chen Tuan agreed and went to the third son, but he did not actually see the son. He only went as far as the door to the son's house; then he turned around and went back to the Emperor.

The Emperor said, "I asked you to go look at my son's face and read his energy to determine whether or not he could be Emperor. Why did you return without fulfilling my request?" Chen Tuan answered, "I went to his house, and I have seen his doorman, servants and workers. Each of them has the quality of being a general, civil official or high minister. If his workers have that quality, that tells me enough about your son. Why should I take the trouble to meet him in person?" This answer made the Emperor decide to make his third son heir to the throne.

Master Chen Tuan stayed in the capital for one month. Then he took leave and went back to the mountain.

Over 100 outstanding scholars of his time came to be his students. Each had his own small hut in the mountain foothills. Day and night they could listen to his teaching. He taught them sometimes at daytime and other times during the night. Although he taught everything else, he did not teach the secret of his "hibernation."

IV

One day, he sent his students to a high spot on the mountain and assigned them to make a hole in a boulder. All his students went with their hammers and chisels and made a hole in the boulder from which one could look down at the clouds, smoke, fog or haze, which from that vantage point looked like the feathers of a green bird with all the vegetation behind it. He told his students, "My lady teacher once told me that I would go through the clouds and enter the high blue sky." After he finished talking, he sat down with crossed legs and asked his students to leave him alone. He used his right hand to support his chin, and closed his eyes. That was during his 118th year. His students returned the next day and stayed around him in a circle, keeping his body protected for seven days, which is the total length of time it takes to complete exuviation. Even after seven days, his face still looked alive, and his body was soft with good fragrance. They made a stone box with a stone lid to keep it in, and bound it with iron and steel chains and kept it inside a stone room. After his students left, a big stone fell down and blocked the entrance to the ravine in which the box was kept so no one could return there. Five colored clouds sealed the entrance of the valley. For months it was not disturbed. Later, people named the ravine after him, calling it "The Valley of Master Shi Yi." This is another respectful title given by the Emperor of Sung.

Much later, during 1119-1124 A. D., a spiritually achieved person came to Hua Mountain. He saw that the iron chain had dropped away, so he went into the stone room. He saw the bones of Chen Tuan in good color and with good fragrance. The man reported this to the new Emperor, who wished to bring the bones to the capital for worshipping. However, when they went to get them, they only saw clouds and fog, which covered the ravine in layers; nobody could reach it. After that, nobody saw any signs of Master Chen Tuan again.

Someone once wrote a poem about Chen Tuan's life.

Some people use a spiritual lifestyle to earn
the respect of others.
Few people like Master Chen Tuan
truly have no interest in worldly glory.
He hid himself on two famous mountains
to enjoy the dignity of natural life.
Four times he abandoned the honor
Emperors wished to offer him.
Nobody knows the Five Dragon practice of hibernation.
The mystic power of the Ba Gua diagrams he received
was sought by many young people.
Numerous pieces of white clouds covered up the ravine.
He lies on the stone bed and has the respect
of thousands of years.

V
Commentary on the Life of Master Chen Tuan

Master Chen Tuan was naturally born with psychic potential. This type of birth can be found in different generations, but he was helped specifically by a teacher with special achievement.

In ancient China, some women who did not choose family life and chose a spiritual path of life hid in a rural place or in the mountains. They gathered feathers and the fur of animals to make clothing for themselves. Wearing this type of clothing, they looked uninteresting to any desirous man. They never let people know where or how they lived. It is known that they used herbs and vegetation to sustain their lives.

The teacher of Master Chen Tuan was one of these women. Nobody knew her name but people called her the Feathery Woman. That name describes the clothing she wore; it means furry or feathery lady.

In Chinese history, when the Yellow Emperor fought the barbaric Chih Yueh, his mission was to protect the ordinary people. He suffered defeat and difficulties, so he sought out helpers, advisors and teachers. It is said that one of those teachers was a woman with a human head and a bird's body.

Basically, she was a type of person like "The Woman with Feathery Clothing." She was called "the mystical female" and she taught Yellow Emperor many important spiritual practices that could help him attain wisdom to solve any possible trouble that might arise.

Because she lived so long ago when people were more open minded, the mystical female of the highest or the Ninth Heaven who helped Yellow Emperor became a spiritual image or symbol. That was around 5,000 years ago. Around 1,000 years ago, during the time of Master Chen Tuan, the Woman with Feathery Clothing was a woman who had an image similar to the mystical female of ancient times. These women were highly developed spiritually but they did not totally abandon the world after achieving themselves. Although they were not directly involved with worldly struggle, they offered a good example by coming to advise others, such as the mystical female who came to help the 16-year old Yellow Emperor.

Although she did not wear unusual clothing or have an unusual body, Mother Chern taught several important students who helped the world during a time of suffering and trouble. Mother Chern lived in a city. She learned her practice and how to use herbs from Master Lan Chi who was a family man with a big family of many generations. She also learned from Prince of Sun who came from the stars as her spiritual child.

The Woman with Feathery Clothing who came to help Master Chen Tuan in his childhood guided him to study the *Book of Changes*. After the decline of the Tang Dynasty (618-906), many ambitious people of military strength competed fiercely for leadership. Sometimes one would succeed and remain on the throne for a short while, but then the fighting would start up again, so from 907 to 960 A.D., people suffered the insecurity, instability and burden of continual war. These wars and the subsequent establishment of the five short dynasties brought much suffering and loss. This period of time in Chinese history is called the Five Dynasties After the Decline of Tang (907-960 A.D.).

During this time, Master Chen Tuan developed himself from his spiritual cultivation through concentrated study of the *Book of Changes*, *The Tao Teh Ching* and *The Teachings of Chuang Tzu*. These three books were called the Three Scriptures of

Mysticism. Master Chen Tuan, who had read many Chinese books, discovered that only those books carried the essential perpetual truth.

Master Chen Tuan knew how to apply his psychic capability of foreknowledge and used it only at the right times. He knew not to abuse himself by giving advice to undeveloped or incorrect people who had unworthy ambitions. He ignored people who might try to use him for his psychic capability; he did it by pretending to fall asleep. Master Chen Tuan was famous for his sleeping. He did not sleep the way most people did, but he had learned how to control his vitality.

Many spiritual people, after they are achieved, act like foolish or crazy people, or simpletons. That was a way of protection for an achieved one who continued to live in general society. Master Chen Tuan used the technique of falling asleep and thus avoided unnecessary problems in his life. Mostly he did not help people because their motives were not high enough, but occasionally Master Chen Tuan would choose to help someone he thought was worthy.

During his time and in subsequent generations, some unachieved people wished to pass themselves off as sages or spiritual people and would act like simpletons, too. This is why, since ancient times, it was difficult to distinguish a truly achieved person from a pretender. Because spiritual achievement cannot be seen, they looked similar from the outside. There were a lot of pseudo-achieved ones and there were a lot of students who went to learn from these impostors. This was the real source of confusion in Taoist and other spiritual teaching.

Master Chen Tuan was a typical sage and achieved one who had great humanistic love. He never really abandoned the world. During wartime, he traveled everywhere looking for people who could become saviors of the time. He knew the subtle law and only helped the right people do the right thing at the right time. He knew that only with those criteria could something be accomplished, especially a big task like saving the world from war.

It was his subtle guidance that helped direct the two brothers to fulfill their task of saving the world from great trouble and bringing peace to the land. He saw their potential and began to guide them, even though they were young. Subtly, on different occasions, he continued to guide the growing young men to direct their energy to save the world during that troubled time. Practically, the Sung dynasty was a play or historical event subtly directed by Master Chen Tuan. Master Chen Tuan could not directly do the worldly task; he could only find somebody who was interested in the world who would fulfill the common wish of all people: to have peace. Master Chen Tuan assisted people who could forget the danger of risking their lives to accomplish the worldly mission of their time.

Master Chen Tuan, as the sleeping sage, not only built up new political leaders, he also taught, and his direct students had a cultural influence for a long time during the Sung Dynasty. They helped people keep their focus on cultivation rather than become lost in any religion. Another record states that Master Chen Tuan was a friend of Master Lu, Tung-Ping, the initiating Master of the School of Golden Immortal Medicine.

Typically, when people become more religious they become less spiritual. Becoming spiritual means attaining spiritual clarity to assist the balance of life. On a big scale, it means that you not only do something helpful to yourself, but you also do something helpful for the world. Religion is only the transformation of selfish desire to go to a mythical Heaven. It is not as truthful as spiritual development. It was a psychological approach, emotional dependence and inertia of evading work on one's own spiritual development.

Following the teaching of Chen Tuan, the Chinese culture philosophically came to a new epoch. His teaching also helped develop the Wu Tan School of physical movement. It is part of the spiritual or internal school of martial arts. It was founded on Wu Dang Mountain where Master Chen Tuan had stayed, by two masters with the same name, Master Tsan, San Fong.

In this school, the Confucian scholars opened up and began to combine spiritual teachings in their study. Although a new spiritual attitude and direction was started which had a long influence - until the beginning of Ching dynasty (1600-1911 A.D.) - the fruit was bitter. Why? Unfortunately, the rigid minds of Confucian scholars mostly combined the faith in spiritual cosmology with the old Confucian teaching. Previously, Confucian scholars usually made study only a tool to hunt governmental positions. Now the new influence made Confucianism into a sort of religion and thus they could find satisfaction in their lives by practicing Confucianism without looking for governmental positions. Thus, the Chinese culture became even more stiffened than before. The natural organic condition of society or general individual life suffered suffocation from the new Confucianism. The Confucian scholars' reception of the spiritual teaching represented a positive influence of Chen Tuan's teaching but the result was so negative because of the twisted-minded later scholars who were crazy about Confucius.

For example, one of the guidelines of Confucius' doctrines was that widows could not remarry. Thus, under the new Confucianism widows could not marry but would typically starve to death, for they had no labor training to work in the field. The initiating spirit and creative incentive of life was all restrained and suppressed by the new culture until Dr. Sun Yat Sen's revolution. After his revolution and its downfall by the communists, society did not change much; Confucianism was only replaced by Marxism. The content of the two "isms" is a little different, but control, rigidity and stiffness still bound the people's souls. Under communism, however, widows can remarry.

My teaching is to respond to the spiritual cultural problem of China, not the political problem. My devotion seeks to respond to the challenge of the stiffness and rigidity of the entire human society. I can only guide people to restore their original, initiating, creative spirit of life through the study of original spiritual learning. The true liberation of people's souls still depends on people adopting natural inspiration for themselves without being entrapped by old or new dogmas.

I give the practice, symbols and diagrams which the Woman with Feathery Clothing gave to the young Chen Tuan in the book *Mysticism.* I wish that through the same way you might also find the clue or the practical inspiration to develop yourself. It is not necessary to be a savior of a time, but at least be a model of a balanced life. In this way, you can help yourself and help the world.

It was Master Chen Tuan's achievement to integrate the teaching of spirituality with Confucius' teaching. By his spiritual influence, all Confucian scholars of the Sung Dynasty seriously continued to develop this neo-Taoism or neo-Confucianism by following his direction. It was thus a new time for reintegrating

Confucianism with Taoism. Naturally, the new philosophy also absorbed the teaching of Zahn (Zen) Buddhism. It was derived from the teaching of Lao Tzu and Chuang Tzu rather than culturally bending one's spirit to religion.

In Chinese history, many people have come forward whose declared vocation is to save the world from trouble. Usually they make lots of noise and accomplish little. Some people consider that they are saviors of their time, but actually they create a great disturbance and pull the world backward. Master Chen Tuan was a person who quietly fulfilled what he thought needed to be done by someone. After success, he never claimed credit. Success or no success, he always abided with the nature within. Tsan Tsai was a scholar and one of the third generation of Master Chen Tuan's students with a reputation in Chinese philosophy and history. He wrote a few lines to express his personal spiritual ambition.

> *Be the heart of Heaven and Earth.*
> *Find survival opportunity for all people.*
> *Continue the wisdom already lost of the ancient times.*
> *Open a new peaceful epoch*
> *for 10,000 generations to come.*

This was written by Master Tsan Tsai, who was stating his own purpose of life. I have quoted him to describe the great personality of Master Chen Tuan who as an active sleeping sage helped create 300 years of peaceful time.

We were born much later than Master Kou Hong and Master Chen Tuan. We can appreciate Master Kou Hong as a bridge for many people who can choose to move from one world to another - from the world of glamour and vanity to a world of quietude and eternity.

We appreciate Master Chen Tuan. His personality was like a ladder. Few people can use it to climb from the narrow ground of earth to reach the vast blue sky.

Master Kou Hong is someone that many people can identify with in their cultivation, myself included. However, I find that the best way to go forward is to take continued support from the study of the *I Ching*.

Chapter 2

Chen Tuan, Master of Immortal Truth

In the history of Chinese philosophy, Master Chen Tuan is the one who laid down the foundation for the new philosophical vision of the Sung Dynasty called neo-Confucianism or Neo-Taoism. Confucius tended to focus upon order within the government or rulership. At this stage of cultural development, the dominant class of agricultural society widened. They developed their range or vista from talking only about serving government and being filial sons and daughters to talking about mind, nature and the universe. Usually that was the subject of Taoists, not Confucianists.

In the history of Chinese Taoism, Master Chen Tuan also had an important position. He was considered to be highly achieved spiritually and some later religious Taoists consider him to be their holy ancestral immortal.

Master Chen Tuan was born in 871 A.D. and ascended in 989 A.D. His other name was Tu Nang. The second Emperor of the Sung Dynasty called him the "Master of Subtle Reality." He was born near the end of the Tang Dynasty, when many ambitious people engaged in military adventure to compete with the new Emperor.

According to one book or record, nobody knew how Master Chen Tuan was born. This book said that once a fisherman lifted his net from the river and found something very big, wrapped in purple cloth. It was as big as a ball, so he took it home. He was ready to cook it, but thunder and lightening kept circling the home. The fisherman was scared, so he took the thing out and threw it on the ground. The purple cloth broke open and a baby was seen. The surname of the fisherman was Chen, so Master Chen Tuan took that surname. We do not know how true this story is, but one thing we know is that Chinese people often have a fantasy that a holy or respectful person must be born into an upper class or good family. However, this story tells us that Master Chen Tuan's birth was not as noble as most people thought.

In his youth, Master Chen was already familiar with the Chinese classics and the teachings of the great scholars before him. By the age of 15, he had already learned mathematics and herb formulas in addition to his regular studies. He also followed the conventional way of taking the governmental examination, so that he could rank among the nobles and rulers. At the time that Chen Tuan wished to take the governmental examination, he was already famous for his knowledge as well as his poems, so all the high governmental officers already knew his name and were anxious to meet him. Many people thought it was a good opportunity to meet the young poet when he came to the capital. However, at this time, the disorder of the military riot started. This destroyed Master Chen Tuan's hope to travel to the capital and take the exam. Since then, the path of his life changed drastically. He decided to give up the ordinary way of life to achieve himself spiritually rather than rank among the nobles and rulers. He went to stay with people who lived in the mountains to cultivate themselves as shiens. He chose a path of spiritual liberation.

During this period, he deeply enjoyed the beautiful mountains and lakes. He met some truly achieved ones and received instruction from them. They told him that the Rock of Nine Rooms of Wu Tang mountain was suitable for his spiritual cultivation. So Master Chen gave up family life to stay there and do his breathing exercise. He avoided eating ordinary food and lived as a hermit on Wu Tang mountain from 934 to 936.

From 937 to 944, he went back to Szechuan Province where he was born to look for a certain person of spiritual achievement who could teach him how to control the breath through controlling the muscles of the nostrils. He heard that there was a master who could transform the internal essence by breathing. This master would lie down, touch the pillow, sleep for months and then wake up. Master Chen Tuan was interested in that and wanted to learn it. The master's achievement seemed to make his worn-out and old-looking skin quite similar to an insect that has left its shell; he was like a baby with fresh skin again, and his achievement made his bodily movement light like a spirit. This was a true profound attainment of internal alchemy.

Chen Tuan was not a man to forget the troubles of the world and go sit in the mountains just to escape. Although he was spiritually achieved, he was interested in helping the world.

Sometimes when he was young he thought, if I cannot be an immortal, I must be emperor. Practically, the teachings of different spiritually achieved ones greatly broadened the range of spirit of the young Chen Tuan.

Although he could not forget the world, he looked for someone else who had the suitable type of energy to be a worldly leader and who could achieve the purpose of bringing about world peace. He traveled everywhere to find such people and instructed them to make an effort to create a new epoch of peace. At the same time, he was looking for someone more achieved than himself for higher instruction. He understood society and knew the trouble of people. He understood the way to return the world to peace. His hope was to build some younger people who had strong energy.

People had already heard about this hope. Emperor Shih Tsung thought that Master Chen Tuan must have excellent talent, so in the year 956, he summoned him to the palace. Actually, his purpose was to examine Master Chen Tuan to see if he had any possible ambition of becoming emperor himself. Master Chen Tuan wrote the following song to Emperor Shih Tsung (954-958 A.D. reign).

Your servant loves sleep.
For my sleep I do not need a mattress or a comforter.
A piece of stone can be my pillow,
  and the grass can be my mattress.
When the thunder scares everything,
  I am your servant who is still asleep.
If I have time, I will think about Master Chang Liang
  who was achieved in the Han Dynasty.

When I feel displeased I will think of Fang Li
  who was also a wise man, spring and autumn.
You talk about heroes, new leaders like Mung Teh
  and Leiu Pei, in the time of three kingdoms.
Those people fight for nothing.
They are not worthy like your servant who lives
  on the top of Green Mountain.
You can find me in the heap of white clouds.
I am really happy.

You can see that my eyebrow is always opened up,
   it is never furrowed like the people with
   lots of worries.
I never need to frown.
I am relaxed, so I enjoy a good sleep.
I do not mind the moonrise or the sunset.

With this poem, the Emperor understood Master Chen Tuan was not ambitious for power nor did he wish to steal his throne, so he let him go home to the mountain. However, because the Emperor was still not totally relaxed, he instructed local officers to watch or spy on Chen Tuan to find out what he did.

When this Emperor died, Chen Tuan took action. Riding a white mule, he led an army of several hundred young people from the mountain villages. They wished to enter the capital to erect a new peaceful center. On the way there, Master Chen Tuan heard that someone he supported had now become Emperor. He was so happy he laughed and fell off his mule, saying, "Now we shall have peace." He did not go to join the ceremony of the new Emperor's enthronement, but he entered Hua Mountain and became a serious practitioner of spiritual cultivation. He fixed up an old Taoist temple from the Tang Dynasty in which to live. The new Emperor, Sung Tai Tzuu (reign 960-975 A.D.) invited him many times to come to the palace, but Master Chen Tuan refused and would not go.

People view things differently. Some people viewed Chen Tuan as the highest, so no one could compete with him in understanding world problems. However, once he knew someone else could handle the world problem, he would step aside to seek his own pleasure in a natural life and forget active interest in worldly power. He was looking for a home in the spiritual world. That is what he did.

The first two Emperors of the Sung Dynasty respected Master Chen Tuan greatly. During the reign of the first Emperor, one important decision made by the new Emperor actually came from Master Chen Tuan. The new Emperor knew what types of things caused trouble in the world. There were many generals who commanded armies and had lots of weapons and great military force, thus they could be the source of disorder. The first Emperor had achieved his own position by being a general who commanded a group of other generals who led different armies. Now that he had become Emperor, he knew that some generals would become stronger and others would become weaker. If the military force was in the hands of a strong man, the world's trouble would not change. How could he take back or revoke the authority of those military leaders?

One evening, after the Emperor finished his daily work, he had a wonderful feast for all the generals and powerful soldiers. Everybody greatly enjoyed it and drank lots of wine. Then he started to talk. He said, "It is difficult to be Emperor. At night, you cannot sleep from worrying about all the kinds of trouble that might arise. At any time, a military riot could start somewhere. It is not as happy a life as that of all you generals who can sleep well and be peaceful because you have no worry."

In response, the generals all stood up, and said, "We vow to offer our loyalty to you, even to die for you."

What did he say? "I am not worried about you. I am worried about those beneath you, the secondary generals who wish to become noble, wish to become dukes, and then start trouble. What shall we do about them?" He told the generals, "We live in the world; the most enjoyable thing is to have some wealth, own lots of fields and have a few nice houses. This will make your descendants feel secure, so that generation after generation, there will be many good things to enjoy until the end of life."

He continued, "I am your Emperor, but I would also like to become your in-law. Our sons and daughters can marry one another, and nobody will ever need to worry about anyone else needing this position." His talk hinted that he was worried about them and subtly made all the generals realize that the Emperor wished to do something about them, maybe to stir up the secondary generals against them.

On the second day, all the generals came back, saying, "We do not like this job any more. We are going home to enjoy ourselves." Then they gave up their military power or command and chose to become rich retirees.

This is a famous story that describes how the generals willingly and readily gave up their military command. Legend has it that it was advice from Master Chen Tuan that helped bring about this period of peace. In that way, they did not need to compete to see who was stronger again, and thus who would be the next Emperor. It prevented a continuation of what had happened during the past five dynasties, where one general would conquer the other, making so much trouble for everyone in the world. One good meal made every general give up his power and authority to command the troops, and just go home.

After the first Emperor died, the second Emperor, Sung Tai Tsung (reign 976-997 A.D.) took the position. Chen Tuan was invited by this Emperor and went twice to give him important suggestions. In 977, Master Chen Tuan was requested to come to see the Emperor. The Emperor asked him, "What is the way to help the world so that people can enjoy their lives?" Chen Tuan could not avoid offering advice, so he asked for brush and paper and wrote four words: "Far, Near, Light, Heavy." The Emperor did not understand. Master Chen Tuan explained, "'Far' means from many places, even far away, invite capable, virtuous people to help you. 'Near' means watch people in your surroundings who would try to please you to hunt for unjust favor; those people will be your trouble if you do not guard yourself from their cunning intentions. 'Light' means tax people lightly. 'Heavy' means heavily reward the soldiers who maintain the peace among people." When the Emperor heard this, he became enlightened and happy. He made these four words the principles of his rulership. Every word really touched the point, capturing the essence of ruling and the success of good rulers over thousands of years. You can see that a spiritual student and achieved person, although he had no worldly ambition, had deep concern for the world. Otherwise, how could he have such knowledge?

Years later, he was invited again. This time, the Emperor asked advice about choosing an heir to his throne. This story was told earlier in this book.

Whenever Master Chen Tuan stayed in the capital, the Emperor invited him to the palace many times to talk about his achievement and his learning of the integral, spiritual truth. He talked to the Emperor about many things, all connected with the profundity of achieving Tao. Their talk was broad, because the second Emperor as well as his brother, the first Emperor, had spent many years in the army and did not have much education, so they appreciated Master Chen Tuan very much. Master Chen

Tuan offered deep instruction to them because he hoped they would be excellent rulers and maintain peace in society.

One day he asked permission to leave, so the Emperor gave a feast and invited all the important ministers. He asked everyone to write a poem to Master Chen Tuan to express their admiration and happiness for what he brought and their sadness in seeing him leave. This made Master Chen Tuan's name highly respected everywhere. Many people, many scholars, wished to become his student. After the feast, Master Chen Tuan wrote a poem and gave it to the Emperor.

For decades my footsteps could be found
in the red dust.
I have missed the green mountains.
They were the only things
which appeared in my dreams.
Colorful clothing and noble position
could not make me feel happy.
Worldly glory is a sort of burden to me.
It was bad news to me each time I heard about a hero
who helped the weakened society.

I do not feel happy about the music
which encourages people to drink more
at the feast when a new dynasty is established.
I would rather take my old books and go back
to the old hut where I can stay by myself.
There are only wildflowers and the singing of birds.
This makes a more enjoyable world
than the one in the capital.

This poem meant to tell the Emperor that his ambition was not to stay in the political arena and that he wished to go away from the closeness to the throne.

Master Chen Tuan's sleep is famous, although it was not actually sleep. He lived as a hermit on Hua mountain. He would stay sleep for more than 100 days before getting up. When the last Emperor, Shih Tsung of the rear Chou Dynasty (961-953 A.D.) suspected Master Chen Tuan of competing for his throne, he locked him up in a room to find out whether Master Chen

Tuan had any ambitions, but he discovered that after a whole month, Chen Tuan was still sound asleep.

Master Chen Tuan's sleep was not the sleep of ordinary people. It is a type of Chi Kung (Chi Gong) called "the practice of hibernating dragon," or "the breathing of the fetus before it is born." Once Chen Tuan described the secret of sleep to one of his students. He said that many people become bewildered from the power of a high position or from the enjoyment of carnal love and that these five words name the things that cause people to become lost in the world. These are name (prestige), money, lust, music and beauty. He said that another four words make them lose their soul: wine, overly rich food, strong drink and the temptation of the opposite sex. Even when they are asleep, they never really sleep because they have so many worries. On the contrary, people who are deeply virtuous and abide with nature refine themselves even in sleep.

Then he gave the instruction for sleep. It means he used sleep as a cultivation to nurture the immortal medicine. This sleep is not ordinary sleep, but it is a time when one's spirit and energy embrace each other. It is a time of deep quietude. When in deep quiet, one can reach very far, reach all the natural energy fields and spiritual fields and go very far.

Master Chen Tuan would lie on his side, and his breathing would be so slow that there was almost no breathing. When many people sleep, they wake up almost like a dead person, but his sleep was full of color and very fresh. For several days or months he would not move. He did not need to eat or drink. He could also make his pulse stop, at least the external pulse. He came to the range of the absolute. This mystical range is not easily described, and it is only understood by those who have experienced it. Master Chen Tuan wrote a poem about it:

The achieved one has no dreams.
His dream is not a dream,
*   it is a voyage to the high spheres.*
The achieved one and even the secondary achieved ones
*   do not sleep.*
When he rests, he nurtures his energy,
*   so the fire in the stove never stops.*
The medicine keeps being refined.

The stove and pot is a metaphor for the body, where there is another world. It is a great secret to find out what happens when the achieved one sleeps.

Master Lu Tung Ping, the friend of Master Chen Tuan, commented on Master Chen Tuan's sleep. He said, "Master Chen Tuan is not asleep; he is a hermit in his sleep. He uses sleep for his internal cultivation. This secret, this truth, can only be told to people who already know how to cultivate themselves. Otherwise, there is no need to talk about it."

So Master Chen Tuan's sleeping practice became the internal practice of the internal alchemists. There are twelve steps, as I explain in another chapter. There were twelve later masters who learned the sleeping practice from Chen Tuan. I include their instructions in the material of the twelve steps.

To sum up the experience of the developed ones who achieved themselves during the Tang Dynasty, Master Chen Tuan himself made some diagrams that show how a person can achieve immortality.

In his diagrams, he first explained the principle that if energy moves from top to down below, it is the way to death. It is what ordinary people do; it is a leak from the bottom. If the energy moves from the bottom and rises, one achieves oneself. This expresses the principle of the cultivation of immortality. In general, people use their essence for their descendants, their children. In contrast, a practitioner of spiritual cultivation stops that leak of energy from the sexual organs and moves the energy in reverse; from down below, the cultivator brings the energy up to achieve immortality. Chen Tuan gave some diagrams to explain it. The diagrams would distract from the information of Master Chen Tuan's life if they were put here. Those who are interested should read my book, *Mysticism: Empowering the Spirit Within.*

Master Chen Tuan said that there are five steps to achieve immortality. The first step is find the secret chiao. Chiao means cavity, the special point, the secret orifice. It is located inside the body cavity. As I see it, he was describing the high subtle energy produced by the cavity of the body.

The second step is to pacify or refine your mind. The mind, if not controlled or disciplined, will become a traitor. You will not achieve anything, then because your mind will become wild and keep wandering. It will keep projecting itself to this and that interesting subject. This kind of wandering never finishes, because practically the mind is also energy. Any thought issued is energy issued. In cultivation, this must be avoided.

The third step is the harmonization of the body and the spirit, or the body and the mind.

The fourth step is to gain immortal medicine.

The fifth step is the nurturing of a new life, a new inner life. This new life becomes ready to be born.

Then after following these five steps, finally you can give up the old shell of the body. The new life is born from the material of existing life. These are the five steps.

To summarize them, the first is to build the foundation. The second is to refine the sexual energy to become energy or vitality. The third is to refine the vitality or energy to become spirit. The fourth is to refine the spirit to become nothingness, because when the spirit is active, knows something or does something, it is still related to the world or to the body sphere of life. When the new being comes, nothing can describe it. The new being comes complete as the new life and is no longer related with any mental or conceptual activity. Otherwise, you still live on this side and do not live on that side. The fifth step is the return to infinity.

The teaching efforts of Master Chen Tuan, combined with those of Master Lu Tung Ping, founded the principles for the new immortal school (it was the old practice with new promotion), the School of Golden Immortal Medicine.

I would like to repeat the guidance and description of Master Chen Tuan's sleeping practice. This is the way he described it; please understand that it was metaphoric.

> *The highest achieved one's sleep*
> *   is within the golden breath.*
> *Intake the jade liquid; the golden gate*
> *   is closely shut and cannot be opened.*
> *The earthly window also is shut,*
> *   and also cannot be opened.*
> *The green dragon guards the green palace.*
> *The white tiger calmly stays in the west room.*

The true energy, true chi, moves
  and generates in the red pond.
The godly water circulates within the five interiors.
This is using sleep to refine oneself,
  to accomplish the great internal medicine.

Master Chen Tuan lived joyfully in the Hua mountains. Every day he enjoyed the breezes and the bright moon. He felt fine above the clouds and beings. He reached the highest pleasure of spirit. Once you reach such happiness, it cannot be described, because your spirit transcends all things. His life being was almost embodied within the clouds and within the haze of the mountains, but he kept deeply within the root of the high spiritual source. In this way, he refined himself.

He had good friends like Master Lu, Tung Ping and Master "Linen Garment" (whose name was not given, but who wore linen garments year-round) and developed a system of physiognomy. They encouraged one another in deeply exploring the spiritual realm.

Master Chen Tuan's study was based on the mysticism of the *Book of Changes*. The purpose of his doing that was to find the secret of the universe. By his attitude in explaining the *I Ching*, he started a new epoch, a new direction for the philosophical approach of the Sung dynasty. In other words, he helped create the philosophical development of the Sung Dynasty.

After Master Chen Tuan discovered the wonders of the mind, he thought that all human creations, including religious faith, theology, or any kind of philosophy were one expression of the natural mind. The natural mind is a product or fruit of the natural self. Through certain individuals, such thoughts, faith and exploration are expressed. However, the essence of a natural mind as the source of all mental and spiritual capability was painted over by the worldly culture. In other words, after people's minds and beings were decorated, painted and covered by the colors and dust of worldly culture, the real nature of the mind could not be known any more.

Chen Tuan also challenged traditional Confucianism. For generations, Confucian scholars had studied the words describing the hexagrams of the *I Ching* rather than trying to understand the energies represented by the hexagrams. This became their limitation. Chen Tuan's approach was different. He thought, if we learn the *I Ching*, we need to learn how Fu Shi himself discovered yin and yang. A mind can trace back to his mind in order to know the high truth. Although Chen Tuan was a scholar, he was not superstitious like most scholars. Chen Tuan did not idolize Confucius; he dared to cast disrespect upon the fashion of typical scholars who accepted the authority of both ancient sages, the Duke of Chou and Confucius. He thought that all those scholars did not look into their most natural mind, by which all people can find the same essence all great sages possess. One must find one's own essence of mind to liberate one's own spirit.

His attitudes were attacked for generations by Confucian scholars of his time until the Ching dynasty. However, he did influence the scholars of the Sung dynasty.

The spirit of Master Chen Tuan became a guiding light of the new cultural direction of the Sung dynasty. The skepticism he cast on the thoughts of Confucian scholars led to cultural and spiritual revolution. This revolution led to two great achievements. One was the development of internal medicine. The other was to clear up people's misunderstanding of internal alchemy. Before, people were superstitious or confused; they trusted the lasting nature of metals and made a medicine from them for the pursuit of immortality. Master Chen Tuan found the truth of spiritual immortality. His way of correcting the misbelief about using metals was to give his own teachings and ignore the topic of metals altogether.

Another thing Chen Tuan did was to lead the existing philosophy toward neo-Confucianism or neo-Taoism, toward finding the truthful spiritual essence of natural life. He knew that the quality of the mind is a natural production and that nature has the capability to produce the high essence. God is related to the high essence of the mind. His new thoughts opened a new path, a new route for the scholars.

Master Chen Tuan divided the knowledge of the *Book of Changes* into two spheres. According to Master Chen Tuan, there were also two different ways to divide or apply the *Book of Changes*, according to the two different spheres of life: Pre-Heaven or spiritual and Post-Heaven or earthly. His understanding was that the ordinary scholars studied something that already existed. This is called Post-Heaven. Thus, their study is the *Book of Changes* of the Post-Heaven stage. He established the *Book of Changes* of the Pre-Heaven stage.

Chen Tuan's focus of study was different in this way. Because the *I Ching* was a book that tried to explain the pattern of the existing phenomena of nature, it was not interesting to him. Thus, his focus was: what about the energy that exists before nature exhibits itself? That is called the Pre-Heaven stage. Thus, Master Chen Tuan worked on the sphere of Pre-Heaven, the wordless message of the *I Ching*.

Pre-Heaven and Post-Heaven can be further explained. Whatever you can see, such as all things in the room, furniture, pictures, your body, the lamp, books, and whatever you can see outside, the mountains and trees, water, whatever, all is called the existence of Post-Heaven. All those things already exist. In the Post-Heaven stage, the law of yin and yang exists. Yang and yin mean high and low, hard and soft, bright and dark, male and female. It includes all dualistic development. Everything pointed at can produce the opposite, contrary thought or object which balances and accomplishes it at the same time. This is called the reality of Post-Heaven.

Master Chen Tuan said, there is nothing to study about the existence of Post-Heaven because everything is there. More valuable is what exists before everything is here; how the universe developed, and what is the reality. His focus is interesting; it is the study of the reality of the stage of Pre-Heaven. Nothing exists in that stage. Master Chen Tuan did not stay with the study of the worded *I Ching*, but he studied the depth of how the *I Ching* developed, which can be explained only by diagrams and pictures (please read the diagrams and my interpretation on the diagrams in the book, *Mysticism: Empowering the Spirit Within*).

Some people might ask, if nothing exists in Pre-Heaven, then from where does everything come? In western religion, the Jewish Bible contains the theory of Genesis, which is the creation story. In Genesis, God already existed. At least, there was the human concept that God existed, but what existed before God existed? There must be a deep root that can be found. That was the focus of Chen Tuan.

It is also interesting that Chen Tuan continued to use the *I Ching* as a **tool for its principles which underlie the words**. Most scholars study the ancient words; they study hundreds of volumes of the ancient study, looking at the interpretation of Post-Heaven reality. Chen Tuan's understanding was that Post-Heaven was so obvious that it did not need to be studied. How about the reality of Pre-Heaven? How can it be expressed and communicated? That is an important thing.

Master Chen Tuan said that in the range of Post-Heaven, there are still levels. There are still different approaches to express the reality of Post-Heaven. At the beginning, the sages were inspired by nature. Only simple symbols were given by them as an interpretation of what they saw. If one wishes to understand the symbols deeply, the real source is to look for the reality of the Pre-Heaven stage. One can start with pictures and symbols, which are beyond what language can define.

So his achievement of the *I Ching* is really different from that of most scholars. The typical scholars' approach of studying the structure of language and words is an intellectual achievement. In Master Chen Tuan's method, everything is derived from the Pre-Heaven stage and manifests or came down to the Post-Heaven stage. The Pre-Heaven stage is energy. It is the root of all things. Once you find the root, once you have the root, let the tree develop and you will have fruit. You do not have to worry about it. How can you talk about the fruit if you do not even have the root? This is the difference.

Chen Tuan lived in the mountains, and he gave up the traditional educational method to find the freedom of the spirit. This is how he initiated a new philosophy. The contribution of his new philosophy, neo-Confucianism or neo-Taoism, was the rediscovery of human confidence in universal life, which is each individual's spiritual essence. *It did not contribute much to society on the practical level of life, because it was mostly the study of Pre-Heaven.* In that reality of Pre-Heaven, there is no question about whether a thing is moral or immoral. True harmony can be found within the core of the universe itself.

Each scholar has a different language; some describe things better than others. Some find only one small thing and discourse upon that thing alone, like one great scholar who only talked about the emotion of respect. The emotion of respect can reach the spiritual reality of Pre-Heaven. Another scholar only talked about one word: quietude. He believed it was important. A quiet mind is what can reach the root of Pre-Heaven. Those things only explain one way. They talk about it and teach it; sometimes they have a large number of students follow them. Surely they are great scholars, but for true service Master Chen Tuan expressed excellence. As I have described, it seems that he did not contribute much to the practical sphere of life, because he worked on the pre-Heaven to influence the life of Post-Heaven. That is his achievement.

During the Sung Dynasty, the work of translating Buddhist scriptures into Chinese was already accomplished. People already had a thorough understanding of each. Thus, the walls could be broken down which had been separating Confucianism, Buddhism and traditional Taoism. People were looking for the essence of the teaching of the different schools. Master Chen Tuan surely did not have boundaries that separated him from any of the religions. He had his own feature in his thought or belief which made his thinking different from that of any religion. He said that all thoughts, all schools and all people existed in the stage of Post-Heaven.

Chen Tuan discovered freedom from all thoughts. The complete function of mind can be found to be much more useful. Scholars cage themselves by words, within the walls of the lines of academic divisions.

We know that everything exists in Post-Heaven, including schools, thoughts and philosophies. Sometimes different ways of thinking become popular, but sometimes they die off. Just like humans themselves, all beings and things in the stage of the Post-Heaven have life and death. They have a time of prosperity and a time of decline. This has been witnessed and experienced. No one can escape this law. Immortality cannot exist in the Post-Heaven stage. Immortality can only possibly exist in the Pre-Heaven stage. Thus, the three schools, Confucianism, Buddhism and religious Taoism, themselves follow the law of the Post-Heaven stage, of prosperity and decline, birth, growth and death. No one religion or one school is appropriate forever.

If you follow the pattern of Post-Heaven, you also are forced into the same limitation without lasting value. The high value is to achieve the lasting truth. The final truth cannot be found among schools or teachings. Teachings, explanations or pursuits are mortal, something that can become extinct, because they are just thoughts or practices. The truthful reality which is worthy to pursue spiritually is internal development.

The three schools each meet a different need of human life. For example, Confucius talked about social order and the system of marriage. Only a few people can certainly live without the need for being bound to it and still be good people. Was the marriage system and social order not developed by human life itself? Yet, despite the fact that it is developed by human life, the teaching is of Post-Heaven. It only finds utility and usefulness within this stage.

Buddhism is a psychological approach. It appeals to people who have emotional distress, frustration or disappointment. They are interested in emptiness. When someone becomes pessimistic, this person needs to turn away from the trouble of reality to the empty space of freedom. The highest teaching of Buddhism is called peace of mind or nirvana. What do you think peace of mind is based on? It is based on the disturbed mind. The disturbed mind is a worldly experience. It is a production that does not come from Pre-Heaven but from the Post-Heaven life experience. Religions are based on experience of the Post-Heaven. Religion is not an external creation; it is yourself too, because it arose from your needs. (I am talking about the collective human need, not you in particular.)

When we talk about spirituality, we talk about God. God cannot exist apart from the reality of life. Where else could God live? There is no place that exists beyond the reality of life. The expectation of spiritual existence is a psychological demand of life. Practically, it can only be achieved through self-discovery. Then there comes the question, what part can God serve in life? In reality, people make the essence of the Pre-Heaven stage serve post-Heaven when they use their spiritual energy to serve the lower interests of their lives. Only when people's evil is straightened out and righteousness is expressed is God there.

You find the existence of God not only in the pre-Heaven stage, but also in the Post-Heaven sphere of life which is full of contradiction and conflict. If the unity of spirits is God himself, God could not exist only in the pre-Heaven stage, because there are many individuals in the Post-Heaven stage who have unified their spirits. However, the discovery of God is to make the reality of the Pre-Heaven stage serve the reality of the Post-Heaven stage. Everybody is looking for blessings from God. Everybody is also looking for blessings from the external world. That direction is the wrong place to look, because blessings come from inside and move to outside, and from down to up.

I will explain this. To come from the top to down below is to bring the pre-Heaven stage down to the post-Heaven stage. I am talking about something moving down: it is your energy. When it resides in your head, it is mental or spiritual energy. When it sinks down, it becomes sexual energy. Worldly life takes what is on top to serve what is low. Spiritual life and achievement is to move what is the low upward, skillfully and methodically. That is self-spiritual cultivation. From the top going down below is to return to the root. From the dualistic stage of post-Heaven, ascending to Pre-Heaven, you will find the root of immortality.

Master Chen Tuan developed the theoretical foundation of internal medicine. One of his students, Master Zhang Wu Mung (the dreamless Zhang) wrote 10 poems to describe the return to the original reality, the return to the truth. Practically, the poems describe Master Chen Tuan's internal practice.

There were many famous teachers in the School of Golden Immortal Medicine. Although everyone considered Master Lu, Tung Ping to be the initiator, the contribution of the theory of the school was mostly influenced by Master Chen Tuan. He was the core of the school or the theory of internal medicine.

Internal medicine as the truth of immortality was not his discovery. It was a rediscovery and achievement of Master Chen Tuan. In ancient times, the teaching was always hidden in metaphors. Internal alchemy was confused with external alchemy, because internal alchemy can only be taught by using the symbols of external alchemy. External alchemy brought three results or benefits to society. One was the medicinal use of metals. Another was the development of chemistry. Another was to change cheap or base metals into something like gold that could be sold for life support.

Good practices and effective methods of internal alchemy were passed down, but this confused the reality of how the individual could truthfully achieve oneself. To refine this internal medicine, there are still two ways to go: with sexual practice or without it. They are also confused. One of the two leads to the development of sexual Taoism, which believes that having more sex will help one attain immortality. Sexual Taoism is still not the truth; it is just the fantasy of one stage of life. I am not in the position to reveal or discuss those high secrets to people who have not reached maturity of mind and spirit.

When Master Chen Tuan started to learn spiritual truth, he was young. He did not need any external assistance from the opposite sex to achieve himself and become immortal. When Master Lu, Tung Ping started his pursuit, he was already 64. When Master Zhang Tzi Yang started his pursuit he was already 78. Many masters achieved themselves in their old age. There are different practices in achieving oneself, depending upon one's age. If a person is older, one first needs rejuvenation to restore one's internal function. The other way is to do it directly when young. Master Chen Tuan gave the direct way. The instructions given by the other masters more or less confused later students, who thought that the practice for achieving immortality was sexual. It is ridiculous to over-emphasize the importance of sex in achieving immortality. Because they were old men, they needed a different energy to awaken their systems. It was not abuse or indulgence in that precious searching; it was a totally different direction of sex. The ancient secret to assist old age has no need to be discussed here, because everybody who reaches me has a good foundation. The detailed discussion will be shown in the book, *Mysticism: Empowering the Spirit Within.*

There are several diagrams from the *Book of Changes* that were passed through Master Chen Tuan's hands to his students. Those diagrams inspired some excellent scholars of later times. They were all inspired and enriched by Master Chen Tuan's work. They are included in the book *Mysticism.*

One lesson from Master Chen Tuan's life is that you must know what kind of person could make what kind of discovery and what kind of person can produce what kind of teaching. It is important to achieve your own good energy. This is funda-mental. Before you are ambitious to achieve yourself, a certain quality of mind and spirit needs to be attained. I recommend that all students learn from the example of Master Chen Tuan.

Chapter 3

Essential Guidelines
for Meditation and Sleeping Meditation

The Secret Instruction of the Mystical Female Given to the Yellow Emperor (2698 - 2358 B.C.): Yin Fu Ching, or "The Guidance to Harmony with the Unseeable." This piece is a very old spiritual work, much earlier than Lao Tzu's Tao Teh Ching. It was passed down orally until the Tung Dynasty, when a spiritually achieved woman, the Mother of Li Mountain, gave an explanation to Li Chuan, a spiritual student and general scholar. There is some esoteric meaning. I provide the fundamental good understanding.

Section 1 - The Way of Spiritual Unity

1. If one observes the Subtle Way of Heaven and controls its secret laws, all can be accomplished.

2. In nature, there are five types of energy: generating or Spring, fully growing or Summer, transforming or prolonged Summer, astringent or Autumn and withdrawing or Winter. When the five types of energy are in harmonious order within a human being, tiny, invisible but real spirits are produced. These spirits join and strengthen the being. When the five types of energy are in disharmonious order within a human being, disaster will occur.

One who discovers the spirits and understands their functions in life will thrive and become prosperous, healthy, self-sufficient and have better opportunities, etc. The same five energies are in the minds of people; when a person sets them in action in a harmonious way, all spirits are at his disposal and do his bidding, and all things receive benefit from this person.

3. The nature of Heaven belongs also to humankind; the mind of humankind is a spring of power. When the Way of Heaven is established, the course of humankind is thereby determined.

4. When the sky is in disharmony, the stars and constellations lie hidden in darkness. When Earth is in disharmony, dinosaurs

and serpents appear on dry ground. When people are in disharmony, they kill one another. When an individual is in disharmony, the person will suffer death. When Heaven and Earth resume their proper course, and when nature and humankind exert their powers in concert or in unity, all transformations begin without obstruction or occur unimpeded.

5. The nature of humankind is here clever and there stupid; one of these qualities may lie hidden in the other. The nine apertures, the openings of the body to the world, all have spirits. The three most important elements of one's existence - body, mind and spirit - are each centered in a particular area of the body. These centers are called the three tan tien. The spirit of each person may be now in movement and now at rest. The person must receive the harmony of all three in order to achieve unity.

When fire arises in wood, the evil of fire can turn into trouble if not controlled. Once it has begun, it is sure to go on to destroy the wood. Similarly, once any calamity arises in a state, if thereafter movement ensues, it is sure to ruin the peace.

When one conducts the work of self-spiritual cultivation by refining oneself and simultaneously uses one's achievement to assist other people, we respect this person as a Sage.

Section 2 - The Way of Enriching Life

1. For Heaven now to give life and now to take it away is the subtle operation of the spiritual origin. Heaven and Earth are the robbers of all things sometimes; all things are the robbers of humankind, and humankind is the robber of all things. When the three partners are not in a positive order, they rob each other. When they act as they ought to, they become the three Powers. They are at peace when they are in correct order. Hence it is said, "During the time of nourishment, all the members of the body are properly regulated. When the springs of motion come into play, all transformations quietly take place."

2. People think the spirit's functions are mysterious, so they worship the unknown. What they do not know is that what is most spiritual are the things and events of ordinary daily life. This ordinary reality instructs the unity of all spirits and

balances the mind. The sun and moon have their definite cycles which vary seasonally. The leaders of people also have differences in spiritual understanding, and they can be apparently helpful or harmful when they perform.

3. The subtle operation of the "three despoilers" moves invisibly and is unknown to most people. The developed one who knows it strengthens his life by it. People of smallness who do not know it make light of their lives.

Section 3 - The Way of Triumphant Life

1. The blind hear well, and the deaf see well. To use this subtle power of the mind is to derive all that is advantageous from one subtle source. This is ten times better than the employment of a host of physical forces. To do this three times each day and night is far better. This is accomplished by concentration in quietude.

2. The mind is activated by external attraction and dies through excessive pursuit of it. The spring of the mind's activity is in the eyes.
 Heaven has no special feeling of kindness, but the greatest kindness comes from it by its being impartial to everything. The crash of thunder and the blustering wind both come without design. People, through their own development, learn to avoid the danger.

3. Perfect contentment is the spiritual self-sufficiency of nature. Perfect stillness becomes the power of one's mind when one is not disturbed by external attraction. Nature seems to be most self-interested, yet the purpose of its operation is the well-being of the universe. It benefits the entire universe.

4. By the energy within us, we control our life opportunity. Life is the root of death, and death is the root of life. Benefit springs from harm, and harm springs from benefit. One who does not know the subtle interrelation of both life and death, harm and benefit, is liable to sink himself in water or enter into fire or in some way bring destruction upon himself.

5. By studying the phenomena and laws of Heaven and earth, undeveloped people become sages. Studying their timing and subtle energetic changes, developed people become wise. Undeveloped people are afraid of their lack of knowledge; however, developed people find freedom from ignorance through wisdom. Undeveloped people consider their sagacity as an extraordinary attainment; the true person of development and wisdom does not pursue what an undeveloped person values.

6. Spontaneity proceeds in stillness, and so it was that Heaven, earth and all things were produced. Heaven and earth proceed gently and gradually, and thus it is that yin and yang alternate. As one takes the place of the other, change and transformation proceed accordingly.

7. The wise, knowing that the spontaneity of nature cannot be resisted, take action accordingly and regulate it for the purpose of cultivation.

The way of perfect stillness cannot be subjected to numerical calculations, but it would seem that there is a wonderful machinery which produces the Heavenly bodies, the relationship between the energies of the eight diagrams of the Ba Gua, the sixty divisions of energy cycle, the subtle influences of using such spiritual power in avoiding the negative resistance on the earth, and the interaction of yin and yang as they alternate and balance. All these come brightly forward into visibility with the spontaneity of nature.

Essential Guidelines for Meditation and Sleeping Meditation

Now I would like to give instruction for meditation and sleeping cultivation which Master Chen Tuan learned and passed down. This was continued by his achieved students. Although the position of the body in sleeping meditation is different than in sitting meditation, the principle is the same. Sitting meditation is preferred to sleeping meditation, but few people can sit long enough.

Sleeping cultivation is best done while lying on the side of the body, no matter whether man or woman. Lie down on your right or left side.   It is better to lie down on the right side, because lying on the left side would press the heart. You should already be using a pillow, but also place your hand under your head just below the ear as a part of your pillow. If you are lying on your right side, the right leg should be bent and the left leg should be stretched out straight. Your left arm should be lying on the left side of your body.

Sleeping meditation is not the same as sleeping, it is breath control. Allow the breath to be deep, thin and long to totally unite with your consciousness. If you try to do sleeping meditation and you fall asleep, there will be no good effect. If you need sleep, just go to sleep.

There is an important instruction that describes sleeping cultivation which can also be applied to sitting meditation. It is to sink the lung energy to the position of K'an (water) by breathing deeply and gently. K'an is also a name for one of the eight hexagrams; it refers to the lower abdomen or kidney.

Then, the liver energy should be moved to the top of the chest or heart. This is also done by breathing deeply and gently. The liver here means nervous energy. This is called the position of Li (fire). Li is the mind/heart. Li is also a name for one of the eight hexagrams.

Breathing makes both Li and K'an unite in the middle of the body. Then the five energies, which are the energies of each of the five organs, become centered and nurture your life.

Adjusting the breathing will integrate the energy inwardly. Your mind needs to be united with your breathing without any interruption. The mind, which is also called the dragon and your emotion, which is also called the tiger, should always stay in the position called the Middle of the Earth, which refers to the center of the body, close to the stomach. Intercourse, or the union of the tiger and dragon energies, produces immortal medicine.

The twelve steps of cultivation and the Five Dragon Hibernation are the same practices with different names. The steps give good, simple, concentrated instruction for nurturing one's internal immortal medicine.

The first step is called "Subdue the Dragon and Tiger." The original energy in your mind is called the dragon. The original essence in your body is called the tiger. When your spiritual energy is calm, the dragon returns to the water in the lower abdomen. When emotion is forgotten, the tiger stays peacefully in the mountain, which is the head. When these two kinds of energy within you, the faithful dragon and the aggressive tiger, are united and harmonized, you shall enter the rank of immortal.

The second step is called, "Refine your hun and po." This is deeper integration of two kinds of body spirits. Both are the spiritual essence of your life being. The ancient teachers used metaphoric language. They said: "In sand, you find diamonds; that is the Hun. From water, you find crystal; that is the Po. The sun is the Hun - the energy giver of the sky. The moon is the Po - the supporter of the earth. In the sun, you find the source of the moon. In the moon, you find the reflected energy of sun. When both are combined, one reaches the creation of a new nature."

The third step is to attune your true energy. Once the five energies are attuned, they all return to the subtle origin of your life being. By the harmonization of the mind through breathing, you have no desire or thoughts going over the rim. To not have desire or thoughts going over the rim means that your mind is not scattered by thinking about many unrelated things, but the mind is peaceful and quiet. By keeping the mind united with the breathing, your thoughts are not scattered. These two opposites stay in the earth position, the center of the body. Your immortal medicine - the essence of life - is thus produced by the intercourse of the dragon and the tiger, the mind and the breath.

The fourth step is to harmonize the yin and yang. We can learn from sky and earth, which are constructed similarly to humans. The physical being carries what is spiritual; this is called "yin embraces yang." The physical expresses the substance, and the spiritual expresses the function. The foundation of nature consists of Heaven - spiritual energy - and earth. Nature is the intercourse of yin and yang. If you can control the yin and yang energy within, your achievement is nearly equal to that of nature. What is the yin and yang energy within? They are two types of force: intelligence and emotional desires as the dragon and the tiger. They are controlled by the subtle conduction of the spirit which is developed from the mind. There is no longer any struggle of the undeveloped mind to control the yin and yang energy within. The spirit is conducted by the Yee, which is the subtle intention of the mind.

The fifth step is revitalization. The yang chi starts over again from the beginning by restoring the sexual impetus. Restoration or recovery happens by the principle that when the yin becomes too extreme, yang is born. When yang becomes too extreme, it gives birth to yin. It is Kou ☰ (#44, Encounter, meeting together).

Fu ☷ (#24, Revival or Renewal) and Kou are both hexagrams in the *Book of Changes and the Unchanging Truth.* Fu means that the yang energy starts to grow from the bottom. Kou means the yin energy starts to grow; it is the opposite of Fu. When yin reaches its extreme, yang returns. When yang comes to an end, Kou, excessive yin, invades again. The one who knows to attune the internal condition through restoration or rejuvenation will find the truth of immortality of life. In this step, one brings one's energy to the point of being excess yin in order to bring the return of the yang energy. This is how to bring about restoration or rejuvenation. It is maintaining the yang energy which is all-important.

The sixth step is to "Nurture your True Fire." From the quiet stillness, suddenly something generates. You feel it internally. From the low foundation of the body, something generates which you call "fire." It is a change of temperature or a new vitalizing opportunity. The root of fire is water. The opportunity of life comes when yang energy returns. Practically, it means the sexual energy starts to stir. During this time, you need good control in breathing. By control, I mean to breathe very slowly to use the pressure caused by slow breathing. The internal work one's ancestors have done spiritually will be enhanced and adjusted.

There are two terms that describe the specific condition and position of nurturing your true fire. They are "The Root of Heaven" and "The Home of the Moon." The Root of Heaven is the top of the head and the Home of the Moon is the lower abdomen. These are two important positions; one in the head, and one in the sexual organs. Use the sexual energy to support your brain energy, especially to transform it into spiritual energy. This transformation is called "quietly nurturing your true fire."

It is difficult to define spiritual energy, so I will give an example. In doing many things, we need patience, because we must wait for something or someone. The patience that we use to tolerate a situation is spiritual energy. Spiritual energy cannot be described, but it leaves a trace, so you can subtly know it. The trace is the subtle essence of the mind.

The seventh step is to keep watching the stove and the cauldron. Stove and cauldron are ancient terms. The head is called the cauldron or the palace of jade; that is where the true yang energy resides. The lower abdomen or belly is called the stove or K'un house; this is where the true yin energy resides. By regulating your body and mind, the stove and cauldron will be in the right position for the production of golden immortal medicine, the newly integrated energy. What are you looking for when you watch the stove and cauldron? That is to produce sen, the high subtle energy and the golden immortal medicine. Also, what is the right position to keep them in? It depends on total self-control.

The eighth step is "Refine your Spiritual Treasure." The subtle consciousness of life is called a treasure. It is not thoughts, it is the energy that exists before changing into thought. It is a little awakening deep inside. Keep that treasure in your body. Once you make use of it, once it is formed, it is called spirit. It becomes effective and efficacious spirit energy. With gentle sincerity, nurture this spiritual energy; then you will have a great light.

The ninth step is "Tie Your Wild Monkey and Your Wild Horse." You need to subdue the wild monkey, but first you need to control the naughty horse. The wild monkey is the mind; the naughty horse is impulse. When there is nothing in the mind, if one small piece of disturbance invades you, you are aware of it, because the spiritual energy within the mind will experience scattering and weakening. You feel the difference in the amount of your spiritual energy that is present.

There are some other terms for this process of keeping the mind free of disturbance. They are the wash and the bath. Cleansing your mind is called the wash. Purifying your behavior and your conversation in talking is called the bath. Pure or correct behavior or speech helps keep the mind clear. Also, it is sometimes necessary to clean out the cobwebs in the mind.

The tenth step is called, "The Pivotal Point of Immortal Achievement." It describes how to control the immortal medicine and, therefore, your immortal achievement. In your cultivation, when you enter the range of the unseeable, inaudible and intangible, it means you are gathering the energy called immortal medicine. When you awaken from perplexity and bewilderment, it means you are developing expanse or becoming open to expansion. The spiritual child has great power; it can cover the entire spiritual world by its expansion. When it gathers together, it can be contained in a tiny pearl.

Now let us discuss the eleventh step. Once you are expanded and vast, you can independently communicate with spiritual energy. Now you know the origin, now you know the root, so you are coming close to spirit. The origin is the vastness. Once you are unobstructed and open, you can reach anything. By the achievement of having no more doubts or thoughts in your mind, you can immediately find an answer to any question that you have. At this time, you can see through to the truth of life. You are also not bothered by the terms of different religious worship. You know that they do not accurately reflect the truth; they are only attempts to describe the truth of spiritual achievement. There is nothing that can block you. At this time, you are not bothered by the ocean becoming land or land becoming ocean. (This means there is no longer any limitation of time or space.)

The twelfth step is called "To Go Beyond the Range of Life and Death." If you gain the Tao, you ascend; this means you are accomplishing your true life. By breaking through the mystery of life, beyond that, there is the origin where you came from. It is the energy.

Spiritual energy cultivation can be done using the posture of spiritual sleeping cultivation. It can be done during the day or at night, whenever you are free. Or it can be done when your sexual energy or your certain desire is stirred. When your natural desire is stirred, it is time for you to stretch your body and then sit.

This is the instruction for sleeping cultivation: Biting the teeth together 36 times awakens the sen or the many sen in your body. You might also call the sen "spirits." Loosen your clothing, especially if it is tight. Lie down on your side, preferably the right side (but the left is also okay) and close your eyes, but not completely. Use the tongue to touch the palate or roof of your mouth. Bend both knees, especially the lower one. Put one hand into a sword position. This is done by straightening the index and second finger and putting them together straight up, and hold down the ring and little fingers with the thumb. Put that hand over your navel or your sexual organ. With your other hand, also make a sword position, but bend your arm and put it under your head to use as a pillow. You may already have your head on a pillow; that is fine.

Your half-closed eyes watch your nose. In this posture, align the tip of your nose with the sexual organ. If you are a male practitioner, make them be in a straight line. Female practitioners can visualize that there is an energy connection between those two points. Your mouth should be closed. The energy channel on the head should be kept open by internal control. The anus should be drawn up or contracted a little bit. Set your focus inwardly. Control your mind by using visualization to increase the light energy in your body. This is called "The Assimilation of the Sun and Moon."

Do not do anything physically; just lie there. This exchanging of the energy channel from the head and the sexual energy is called "The Union of K'an (water) and Li (Fire)." This is the internal intercourse of the sun and moon.

The principle of energy cultivation used in sleeping meditation is to keep the spine slightly bent like a deer's spine, with slight natural bending. Nurture your energy inwardly like a crane, and breathe soundlessly to survive like the turtle. This energy produced by the circuit of breathing can be long and wide enough to cover an area or distance as big as 84,000 Chinese li, which is about 28,000 square miles.

Internal energy responds to external energy. All external natural energies can communicate with internal functions. Making your thoughts return to be original spirit is internal medicine. When the body is full of internal medicine, it contains an essence which appears as light outside like an aura. By converging internal and external energy to become one, you enter the subtle origin.

When you come to this stage, you must beware of the six thieves. They are the five senses and your mind. When the six thieves are naturally extinguished, then the five elementary energies will naturally come together. Fire and water will then follow the natural order, ascending and descending to brew the true elixir and nurture the spiritual root.

It is said that internal intercourse is connected with all bodily secretions before they become so. When you sleep, your mouth might feel like you are drinking light spring wine; it does not taste dry or bitter.

If you practice doing all kinds of cultivation day and night, your true energy will not be lost. When you finish sleeping and wake up, you can massage your face, eyes and body to make your mind and body happy. Whenever you walk, sit or lie down, use your mind to gather your energy. When the mental energy stays within the body, the spiritual energy also stays. When your spiritual energy stays, you are not bothered by thoughts. Your chi stays, and you will not have panting breath. Panting indicates weakness.

When the spiritual energy stays, your essence stays. When your essence stays, your body is firm and you do not feel like you need sex. Then the three origins - mind, body and spirit - return to be one. Then all the energy channels - the twelve main ones, two general ones and eight extra channels - come back to the source. All your body's energy with its different manifestations will no longer leak. Your blood will change and you shall have good health and longevity. Your eyesight and spiritual vision will be strong.

For successful spiritual cultivation, you need to keep your spirit quiet and your emotions peaceful. If your mind becomes too active, your spirit will become tired and your energy will scatter. When your energy is scattered, your essence will be weakened and your body form will be withered. When your body form is withered, you are going to die.

Worldly people live through life and death like a dream, but the achieved ones are different. They do not have wild thoughts, wild dreams or disturbing desires. Their mind is always clear and free, so their spirit always stays stable and crystal clear. They are beyond coming to life or leaving life, beyond having life or death. Such a life does not enter the cycle of reincarnation.

The minds of worldly people never stop for one second. Their minds and emotions kindle each other and burn up their energy. When the mind is bound by worldly pressures and interests, the spirit has no peace. During the day they dream, and at night they dream. Thus, they dream when they are awake and they dream when they are asleep.

When they come to the last minutes of their lives, they are still attached to desires or emotion, so without any choice, they naturally enter a different kind of life opportunity. They may enter the next life to become a horse, dog, pig or other animal. This is what happens when a person's energy comes and goes and does not stay consistently within the body.

If people cut off the attachment of affectionate relationship, they would not need to follow along the cycle of reincarnation. Now, however, people experience love, desire, greed, anger and stupidity and mistake them for joy. They do not know that false joy is poison. When people cling to false joy, it eventually takes their lives. They think their desires bring them gain, but the result is to kill themselves.

All external attractions steal a person's life energy. All the things we do are created by mind, but the mind is a house of thieves before you develop yourself spiritually. These thieves steal and destroy your vitality.

After you achieve yourself, the natural function of mind is restored. Thus, mind is the house of spirit, and spirit is the master of the body. In general, people take the thieves as their masters and obey them, resulting in destruction of their lives.

Let us talk about cultivation. What do you cultivate? You cultivate no more than the ching (sexual essence), chi (vital energy) and sen (spiritual energy), which are also called the Three Treasures. The sen or spirit is the master. The chi or energy is the minister. The ching or essence are the citizens. These three treasures can be stolen by the thieves through the desires of the senses. If they start to stir, your spirit scatters. If the six thieves disappear, then you have peace. Once you have peace, the citizens - the spirits of the body - are not difficult to rule. They become easy to order, each with its own function. So it is important, externally, to subdue desire and internally to have peace with your spiritual energy. Then you can refine the sexual energy to be chi, refine the chi to be sen and refine the sen to return to the origin. That origin is not definable.

All things return to the three - the original spiritual energy, the original mental energy and the original physical energy, just as they were before they were active and before creation was brought about. Three return to two - yang and yin. Two return to one - unity of the prime energy. One returns to the originally undefined source. This is the path of being a spiritual immortal.

The energy of worldly people follows a different path. Their energy tends to be downward and splitting. Their spiritual energy changes to be physical energy, physical energy turns to be sexual energy, sexual energy gives birth to children. One gives birth to two, to three, to all things. Most people follow the way of life and death. Life and death are the result of the birth of desire in the mind. That is the result of the pursuit of worldly expansion.

This explains the way of the shien or immortal and the way of humans. The way that most people follow is to go downward. The way of the shien is to go upward.

People who nurture spiritual energy have an undisturbed mind. They nurture their mind or their energy like a master nurtures the fetus, like the hen guards its eggs, or like the mother clam takes the light of the moon. Once your energy or your practice reaches its maturity, it is like ripened grain or a melon ready to cut from the vine.

Spirit is the mother of energy, the chi. The spiritual essence is the child of the chi, the energy. When spirit and chi embrace each other, the sexual essence will return to the origin without being scattered. This is how the spiritual baby is born. The secret of giving birth to a spiritual baby is to keep your spirit in the center of the body. By doing so, the two opposite kinds of energy will have intercourse in the yellow court. The three products, ching, chi and sen, will become one in the origin. Your holy womb becomes truth. When this is fulfilled, your true spirit can depart from the range of life and death to achieve Tao.

By keeping the energy centered in the body for one hundred days, you reach the practice of the old-aged turtle which is to nurture your kidney energy or the source of vitality. By doing it for three hundred days, you shall have the foundation of your immortal medicine. By doing it for two years, your body will become light and your mind effective. The top of the head as the meeting point of the thousand energies will open, and the Heavenly eye opens. It takes three years to create the foundation for ascending to reach the unthinkable, unspeakable, undefinable truth. Through your sincerity and constancy, you shall find evidence that this is true.

Chapter 4

Internal Energy Conducting
and Orbit Circulation

I

You need to know about the orbit circulation. Orbit circulation means channeling the energy (chi) upward in the back from the tailbone or perineum toward the crown (the top of the head), then down the front of the body to meet the yin energy in the perineum again. This is the general idea.

This practice is popular among practitioners of spiritual cultivation, but several things may happen unexpectedly to those who practice it. Some people take years to learn how to do it, only to find that the practice causes more trouble than benefit. Others may do it for many years only to find no good result, so the time spent was wasted. Or, somebody might become overconfident and imagine that he has achieved this practice when he actually has not. This person might think he has already achieved something in spiritual cultivation. Then trouble might happen, and he does not know the cause of the trouble. The person may think the trouble has come from something else.

Orbit circulation is a system of practice in achieving immortality. In ancient times, spiritually achieved ones were mostly family people who lived in the world. They knew how to harmonize their sexual energy and utilized correct and proper occasions to do so, but after Buddhism became so popular in China, people began to believe that celibacy was the way to reach Tao. Celibacy was identified as almost the only spiritual path. However, when celibate, many men have involuntary ejaculations during meditation. This is usually called an energy leak. Later achieved ones emphasized orbit circulation as the means to help men stop the leak. Practically, there are many ways of stopping the leak; orbit circulation is only one way. If you wish to do this practice you need to know some important details.

II

When you enter any kind of meditation or when you wish to begin doing the orbit circulation, do not have any preconception or expectation about what should or will happen. For example, some people think that when they meditate, their lower Tan Tien should be warm. That is a preconception; meditation is not experienced that way by everyone. Once you have a preconception - which is not natural - you subtly begin to guide what will happen. Then your achievement will not be natural; it will be forced. If your achievement is not natural, it does not fit the purpose of meditation, which is automatic self-adjustment of the body. The body is Tao; it adjusts itself by itself if you do not interfere. However, people like to interfere and try to make things happen. That is not proper in spiritual practice.

If you do meditation, what you need is a good meditation, so sit there, relax and let the body do what it does according to its own wisdom, step by step. Do not use the mind to command the body or demand something. Preconception is a limitation that will hold you back at one level of experience, even if you are ready to go on to a higher level.

Doing spiritual cultivation in the Integral Way allows for the natural internal course of the energies of fire and water. Mental energy is symbolized by fire, and sexual or kidney energy is symbolized by water. These two kinds of energy perform subtle intercourse to bring about a condition of generating energy. This is accomplished naturally and smoothly by itself if you do not interfere. The energy knows what to do without your needing to tell it what to do.

When you learn the spiritual refinement of internal medicine, the main thing you need to do is respect what you are doing and follow the right way, which is to establish clear-mindedness. Rarify your intentions and desires. Whatever you do, look for harmony.

The most important thing you need as a foundation for the higher practices is to learn Tao. The basic guidance of Tao is the first instruction. Tao is nature; it is self-nature or universal nature. Tao brings evolution. It is universal intention of universal nature that has brought about life and that has brought about your life. There is nothing extra you need to do; you do not need to issue or project your ambitions or motivations. Instead, you need to learn to be calm. By maintaining calmness, you reach true mind and learn to appreciate the source of your thoughts. The source of the thought energy is the pure body of the mind.

Thus, learning Tao means learning how to support a life that is active but also quiet and calm. My other books talk a lot about how to do this. This is the important foundation for higher practices.

Once your life is calm, in your meditation you stay right there. This means do not let your mind be preoccupied. You need to keep your mind unoccupied and keep the energy within. If you keep thinking, you scatter your energy widely or far away in the past or future. Once you maintain the life energy within and reach the deepest root (by not doing anything extra, keeping your purity and staying quiet), then your yang energy naturally evolves to be spirit and true achievement will come. This is the first thing I would like you to know.

III

The method used in orbit circulation is similar to that of cooking or of refining metals, both of which use a stove and a cauldron. I would also like you to know about the concept of internal elements such as the cauldron and the stove.

The stove and the cauldron are important. In ancient times, the cauldron was the receptacle in which the food to be cooked was placed. The cauldron was then put over the stove where the fire was burning. A simple image can be made of a pot holding rice over the stove to be cooked, as it was done in all kitchens at that time.

The cauldron is a cooking pot with a lid which rests over a metal tripod. The cauldron is also a big container in which a sacrifice was to be cooked over the fire. In an ancient spiritual ritual when a cow was killed, and after the sacrifice was dedicated to Heaven by the king, the meat was divided first to the elders and children, and then to the adults in the community. Underneath, a fire was made to do the cooking. When metal or iron was first discovered and put to good use about 4,500 years ago in China, it was an industrial breakthrough and caused a celebration of peace and prosperity in the community. The image of the cauldron became a symbol of something wonderful being prepared through the right process which promised success.

IV

You already know from reading my other books that in the body the mind is fire and the kidneys are water. In the human body, the fire is above the water, therefore you need to turn them around. If you do not turn them around, the fire will reach higher and disappear, and the water will sink and disappear. Thus it was the observation of the achieved ones that people needed to put fire under water for the two energies to work together and produce something useful. When no joining happens, both sides become depleted, which will only finish a person's life sooner.

In internal cultivation, the cauldron, which is usually called the Jade Cauldron, is inside the brain. The cauldron is the center of the brain or the most central energy location. The concept of a cauldron also describes the material to be refined inside the cauldron - in this case, raw energy. I am talking about a receptacle like a cauldron - e.g. an energetic container. Basically, it sounds like the cauldron is the brain itself. The brain is where the mind and the spirit stay.

In internal alchemy, you take the mental energy, or fire, and move it from inside the cauldron to inside the stove, which is the reproductive system of the body, or water.

The Golden Stove is located around one and a half or two inches behind the navel. Let us describe the area of the Golden Stove in more detail. The area around and just behind the navel is called the Spiritual Sanctuary, and the point corresponding to the navel on the spine is called the Vital Gate. The Vital Gate is where physical vitality is generated. On both sides of the Vital Gate, only slightly deeper within the body, are the kidneys, left and right. These four - the navel or Spiritual Sanctuary, the Vital Gate and the two kidneys - are all very close to the physical center of the body. That physical center between those four spots is the Golden Stove.

What you do in your meditation is to place your thoughts upon this physical center of the body, the Golden Stove. Because the nature of thoughts is fire, putting your thoughts in the location of the Golden Stove places the fire under the water. Thus, internal alchemy begins; the inside of your body becomes a place where cooking happens. It could be likened to a nuclear reactor in which energy is being generated.

Be careful about doing this type of energy projection not to go too far back. In the back is the large intestine, which is located just in front of the kidneys. You need to be sure that you put your energy in the stove, not in the large intestine. The location of the stove is about two English inches or 1-1/2 Chinese inches behind the navel. Do not put the fire too far back. If you put energy in the intestines, it is of no use; you will produce energy, but it will be in the form of gas. It is of no benefit to have your bowel full of gas. This is why your focus or fire is put only two inches behind the navel.

Also, if you project the attention too strenuously onto the kidney energy, the 'strong fire' will hurt the kidneys. This will disturb you by stirring you up sexually. This is why you need to be gentle in projecting your mental energy or fire.

Sometime after you have built a strong fire, you need to move your attention deeper, closer to the backbone, to the spot directly between the two kidneys which is called the Vital Gate or gate of life. Energy produced from there will seek an existing route to move upward. After the water energy is refined or heated up by the fire, it becomes vaporized and after you move your attention to the Vital Gate, it ascends up through the spine.

The points we use in spiritual cultivation merely indicate a location where you project your mind to create an energy field to produce the desirable result that your mind commands. The same is true of acupuncture points. Both acupuncture and cultivation cause a response from the nervous system which creates a beneficial energy arrangement that gives physical help or improves the emotions or internal energy. The points are not like a small organ or system that can be located anatomically. Some day, perhaps someone will find something at those points, but finding a physical correspondence is much less important than the real practice of moving the energy to these points. For example, a bee sting or mosquito bite can affect the body. A nuclear leak hundreds of miles away can also affect the body. These are negative examples of how the intervention of different energies can affect the human body. Spiritual cultivation and acupuncture, on the other hand, produce a good result for human life. One way of approaching life is to have a rigid attitude toward understanding human life and nature, but if you are engaging in spiritual cultivation, it is better to keep an open, flexible attitude toward reality.

It is also important to know the two positions of the Sanctuary of Spirits and the Vital Gate. The Sanctuary of Spirits is used during the time a fetus stays in the womb. It is the important connection with the mother through which the fetus receives nutrition and spiritual education, etc. The navel is a symbol of T'ai Chi after the child has an independent life. I wish you would avoid putting your attention there; when you are young, it will attract your sexual energy and make you desirous. Do not mix up the lower Tan Tien with another spot. Tan Tien means where the energy is being produced in the Golden Stove.

In spiritual cultivation, some people concentrate on the back of the spine, others on the perineum, but neither of these points will achieve the desired purpose. The perineum is a gland for men, but not for women; the location is the meeting point of yin energy between the legs. For older people, the perineum has a rejuvenating purpose if their sexual energy has almost died off. However, for real serious spiritual cultivation, one's sexual energy is already in good condition. The perineum is not the choice spot, because it does not have well-blended energy and you cannot produce the pure yang seeds of medicine there. *So using the perineum will not help one achieve the true medicine; it will only help restore one's failing sexual energy.* Typically, once people restore their sexual energy, they like to have more sex, so it is better to focus on the other spot.

In their practice, some people concentrate on the spine. There is lots of benefit to concentrating on the spine, because even if you do not achieve anything, the spine itself, as the center, makes all the nervous connections in the internal organs. When you sit, if you concentrate on the spine, you will be strengthening the nervous system and will live a long and healthy life. What else do you require from life? If you are looking for medicine, and you concentrate on the spine, you will have a strong nervous system. Still, someday, you will need to die. That is okay. Even people who do meditation to achieve internal alchemy die someday, but they experience a different result.

If you focus your cultivation on the nervous system, then when you die, you will not have accumulated enough energy to be able to move away. If your goal is immortality, then you need to accumulate energy by learning to project energy; start by moving it.

The instruction for internal alchemy is first to place the fire in the Golden Stove and then move it to the Vital Gate. Do not place it in the Spiritual Sanctuary or the Tan Tien. Only place it in the perineum or spine if you have a different purpose than immortal practice.

The water or kidney energy is the Post-Heaven energy and the fire or mental energy is the Pre-Heaven energy. When you cultivate the internal energy, the Post-Heaven energy will internally intercourse with the Pre-Heaven energy. This means the water or kidney energy mixes with the fire or mental energy. The original purpose of internal alchemy is to borrow the post-Heaven sexual energy.

Above I have said that the stimulation of the sexual energy comes from the perineum. The sexual power connects with the kidneys to go with the fire of mind to conduct the yin energy of the gathered and combined energy to have intercourse with the energy of Pre-Heaven, which is mental energy with no thought. Here, internal alchemy means the internal secretion produced by the body gland before sexual stimulation is a part of the energy in making the Golden Immortal Medicine.

If the fire energy does not meet the water energy through cultivating the Vital Gate, there is no benefit spiritually for immortality or physically for health.

Q: Master Ni, you have often said that sexual energy is the foundation or raw material of all the energy of the body, including mental energy or the mind. Thus, why is sexual energy considered as Post-Heaven energy and mental energy considered as Pre-Heaven energy? Doesn't sexual energy exist before mental energy?

Master Ni: A correction must be made here. The sexual energy which is increased by sexual desires or sexual activity is newly transformed from the body energy. Thus, it is post-Heaven energy. It no longer remains as original vitality. Mental energy, before any thought or idea or activity is issued, is at the Pre-Heaven stage. If a thought, idea, etc., is issued, then mental energy is transformed to the Post-Heaven stage, the same as bodily energy. Here, Pre-Heaven means original or undisturbed, before being newly formed or issued by the mind. This is the way to distinguish the stages of all energies. The cultivation of immortality does not use the Post-Heaven stage of energy, whether from the mind, chi, or tsing (jing or ching). This is one important part of immortal cultivation. The intake of hormones by mouth or oral sex has nothing to do with immortal cultivation. It is in a different level.

The cultivation of refined medicine first needs the convergence of fire. If you put a magnifying glass under sunlight and put a piece of paper under it, after some time the paper begins to heat up and burn. It is the same thing in internal alchemy; the fire must converge. Your gentle concentration is what gathers the fire. The metaphor of the magnifying glass is important, because it describes the convergence of the focus of the fire onto one spot. You first need to achieve that.

In general terms, it describes mental concentration or the ability to stop mental wandering. Generally, people are scattered. They keep thinking about things, so nothing happens toward their achievement of immortality because their mind focuses differently. The gathering of mental energy as the intention of mind is just as strong as the fire. Therefore, if you keep the fire burning, the concentration of fire must work together with the water energy. It means the original secretion, when it is at the Pre-Heaven stage.

The intention of mind is like a fire which keeps focusing in one direction. As the concentration occurs, it must have purpose and result. If you do not do the refining - by this I mean, if you do not move your attention down to the Vital Gate - so you keep the fire burning in your mind, then your mind starts to be active and all you achieve is a wildly active mind. Then true internal alchemy will not happen. Also, if the location of meeting for the two energies is wrong, such as in your intestine, the result will build gas in your abdomen. In that case, you will cause internal trouble, maybe a lump will grow. Otherwise, if you have a wildly active mind, your energy is just scattered and is eventually exhausted. This is important. You have to do the refinement by proper concentration upon the Vital Gate after the strong fire is built.

Do not be misguided or learn incorrect instruction from someone without truthful knowledge or truthful achievement. If you try everything that other people recommend, even after ten generations you still will not have achieved anything. You have to learn something from someone with real achievement, who can prove it.

The right way of cultivation is to correctly know what is the cauldron, what is the stove (the metaphoric reactor) and what needs to be refined, such as the sexual energy. The cultivation of Tao or internal alchemy is to catch the spirit (the fire or mental energy) in the right spot. After you can concentrate your mind or fire energy on the Vital Gate, then your breathing will change; this will make the mind and the breath naturally follow each other.

There is a difference between a gentle fire and a strong fire. You need to control your mind, i.e., how strongly your attention is projected. A pure mind is needed to observe and supervise the use of fire and wind (breath). By the continual internal burning, slowly sublimation and circulation will happen, and the true growth or true production of Golden Immortal Medicine will happen. Golden Immortal Medicine is a spiritual formalization.

V

I have only briefly mentioned orbit circulation. Basically, orbit energy circulation is a mental energy conducting. It is using the mind to conduct your reproductive energy upward and circulate it along the central line in the front and back of the body, deep in the skin where your nervous system can still feel it. This is done in order to have no energy congestion or stagnation and reform the energy to be new immortal energy.

VI

I would like to explain more about internal alchemy. The two important locations in the human body are the Ting 鼎 or cauldron, and the Lu 火盧 or stove. The ancient spiritually developed ones stated that individual human life is a small model of nature. In nature, the sun, moon and stars are above us, and on the surface of the earth, all types of life are active or less active. In the universe, there are two types of energy. One type of energy is light and moves upward. This type of energy is also called "sky energy." Another type of energy is heavy and moves downward. This type of energy is also called "earth energy." Before language became complicated, they used two symbols to describe these two types of energy: ☰ Chyan for sky energy, and ☷ Kun for earth energy. This was the first step in explaining the whole possible process of nature.

There are two basic possibilities for energy: earth and sky. In human experience, the sky is always above us and the earth is always beneath us. The first possibility is if in any situation, the upward moving energy continues to go upward and the downward moving energy continues to go downward, then nothing will be produced in the universe. However, if the sky energy is sent down to earth and the earth energy is sent up to the sky, then the two types of energy interplay and intercourse. They form a new type of energy: life. This is how all lives happen on earth.

The ancient developed ones utilized the symbol or hexagram of Pi, Misfortune ䷋ , to describe the first type of situation in which the two energies go their own way. Harmony, integration and cooperation are not seen. The ancients used T'ai, ䷊ the hexagram for peace and prosperity, to describe the second situation, where the upward energy moves downward and the energy below moves upward. This new situation expresses harmony, integration and cooperation to bring about a new stage with the creation of life.

These two symbols, Pi and T'ai, are also used to describe good and bad politics. Not all leaders remain above the people. A good society is created when those in the upper position communicate and cooperate with those below, and vice versa.

VII

Now let us come back to talk about Internal Alchemy. If the head energy always stays in the head, and the abdominal energy always stays in the abdomen, there is no communication or transportation. Thus, there is no generation or creation. Only when the head energy moves down to the abdomen and the abdominal energy moves up to the head does an exchange happen. Intercourse happens and inner circulation happens; then, the health of the individual is certain. The creativity and productivity of the person is also possible. Otherwise, stagnation or scattering is seen. This describes the natural situation of each individual life. This concept is adopted and emphasized in internal alchemy.

For example, the head energy is always interested in having more, watching more, enjoying more, stretching more, and going out far. The abdominal energy wants to eat more, have more sex and enjoy more leisure. These two types of energy can present two directions of movement, which can create a situation of separation as each one goes its own way. So the basic guidance of spiritual cultivation is to restrain the head energy - by not being too outward, except for what is necessary and using that energy to support the abdominal energy. You restrain the abdominal energy which likes to have more sex to sustain and support the head energy. Then the integration, cooperation and intercourse happen naturally within the individual.

This not only ensures the health of the individual, it also suggests longevity. This is general guidance and is available to all people, no matter what religion or ideology they hold. We call this the natural foundation of life; nobody can be against it.

The natural type of life is expressed by the hexagram for peace and prosperity, T'ai. In the unnatural type of life, the head wishes to be spiritual and the body would like to have more sex. This type of dualistic practice, done by many general religious followers or people who do any type of extreme practice, is described by Pi. It expresses the unnatural reality of life.

VIII

Now, let us concentrate on internal cultivation. Human life, which is basically like the big nature, consists of two types of energy; fire and water. Fire ☲ is symbolized by Li, 離 beauty. Water is symbolized by ☵ Kan, 坎 entrapment. Fire energy is always moving higher above. Water energy always flows downward. In a situation of unaccomplishment, fire is on the top and water is down below. In expressing the internal situation, the two types of energy go their own way. Only when they are turned around, with water on top and fire below, can perfect accomplishment happen. It is just like boiling water; you need to put the water in the pot and place it on top of the stove. Water will never boil if the fire is placed on top of it.

From these two symbols of natural energy, you have a better understanding of the right way to order one's personal internal energy and practice cultivation.

Cultivation involves some techniques such as breathing. The breath controls how much oxygen comes into your body to help the generation of internal energy. Let us discuss this by referring back to the ancient symbols.

In the *Book of Changes and the Unchanging Truth*, among the 64 hexagrams, there is one hexagram called Ting or the Cauldron. ☲ In the Cauldron, fire is on top and wind is below. This illustrates using the wind or breath to help the burning of internal energy. Like the hexagram, your breathing must be deep to reach the bottom in order to help the generation of the watery energy beneath. Many people who are overweight have deposits of fatty tissue in the lower parts of their bodies. Their breath is short and cannot reach down below. It is important to breath gently, quietly and deeply. This means, the breath must extend into the lower part of the body. By deep breathing, you exercise the lower abdomen by creating internal pressure. The breath is not just done in the chest area. People who are stressed a lot or who are overweight often have trouble doing this.

A long, deep, gentle, quiet breath in meditation, in your concentration, will help the function of the body. It will assist the generation of energy and help burn off stagnant energy, including fat. Correct breathing is one important principle in governing your body. Remember this when you have the problem of slight stagnation. If you have a situation of big stagnation, breathing is not enough.

If we change the order of these two trigrams and put fire below and the wind on top, the hexagram of Cauldron changes to become the hexagram of Family, Chia Jen. ☲ Many people talk about the problem of the family in modern times. Even in most individual people, the internal energies are not united like a loving family, they are more like a group of fighting enemies. Harmony is necessary whether it be among a group of people who live together, or internally within one individual.

In this hexagram, the wind on the top blows the fire to make warmth reach everybody. By warmth, I mean love and forgiveness. Without those two elements, no harmony can be created.

If there is no harmony, there is no family. Notice that in the hexagram, the bottom line or foundation of the family is discipline, regulation or restraint. Each individual applies discipline to himself or herself and then adds the elements of love, care, understanding and forgiveness to bring harmony to all.

We already discussed the relationship between breathing and fire energy within. How about the relationship between breathing and water energy within? If the water energy is on top and the wind energy is on the bottom, it creates an image of the Well, where the energy fountain is located. ☵ The Well, of course, not only describes the place where the energy is stored. If that were the case, it would describe a dead well, something of no use. The well also provides the energy for each faculty of the small community in the individual body. That is the function of the energy fountain. Through breathing, you can generate energy within, like an energy fountain which presents the inexhaustible source.

When wind is on top and water is below, a situation of dispersion is created. This is represented by the hexagram Huan, Dispersion ☴ . In this situation, no stagnation happens within. The wind disperses the water energy or sends the water energy to all. This is a good use of energy.

The above discussion is a supplement to the description of the location of the cauldron and the stove. If you remember these principles we have discussed using the trigrams and the hexagrams of the *I Ching* as general guidance of a natural healthy life, and as the general guidance of your internal energy cultivation, you will be going on the right way. You will meet success, with no need to go into meticulous details. The meticulous details are the result of rigid programs set up by the tendency of secondary teachers or secondary students. If you understand this big principle of bringing the fire under the water and mind under fire, the orbit circulation will be well controlled by your understanding. The localized sensations and feelings are only minor proofs.

IX

When I first came to the United States as a teacher, I met some patients and other people who were teachers of kundalini yoga. They had the same concept or wish to move the sexual energy up to the head. I saw them use lots of strength to try to accomplish this. I do not know what they achieved, and I prefer not to comment on it. However, in the traditional immortal way, if you sit in meditation and try to use physical strength or the mind to rush or speed up the body to accomplish the orbit circulation, this is considered abandoning the Tao to follow your desire. By "abandoning the Tao," I mean you no longer harmonize with your life and with the universe. This is an external forcing and brings empty achievement. You must understand, if you try to force it, once you sit there, sometimes you will feel cold or warm, and sometimes you will see colors or all kinds of shapes. Some people think that this is the goal or good result of their "spiritual" methods, but these sensations are all illusion, all temporary symptoms. The Golden Immortal Medicine is not effective yet. These symptoms are only the obstacle of your mind or of your knowledge.

Q: Do the illusions occur only when you force it, or do you also see things as a result of natural practice?

Master Ni: If you force the orbit circulation to happen, two things occur. One is that you fail to achieve the true Golden Immortal Medicine and achieve illusion instead. Second, the misuse of the mind creates a spiritual obstacle. What does the word 'obstacle' mean? An obstacle is like feeling your head has become heavy; it feels as though something like a big mountain is pressing it. Or it may feel like your head is bound by many wires. Why does this happen? Because you have misled or misguided and disturbed the energy flow, or you have overdone the mental conducting by forcing the energy flow. That gathers all the fire in your head instead of in the Vital Gate.

In learning the orbit circulation, you must follow nature. Allow the true yang energy to go through the possible obstacles, which are several joints of the spine and the bone in the back of the head. Then the yang energy will stay or fly as you choose after you have achieved the smooth transportation and transformation of your refined essence. The natural way is the true way. If you force yourself, command, demand, or wish to make things happen, the original true medicine produced by nature will be lost.   Because there is no real material, this will cause only disorder or internal disharmony.

If you do not follow Tao, the natural path, you had better not be an internal alchemist.   You can enjoy some exercise or whatever.   If you are seriously looking to be a refiner of internal medicine or alchemist, you have to follow nature.   Any slight preconception, slight imagination of mind, or slight forcing, is really not true achievement.   It is really not the way.

The correct way is when your spirit - the fire or mental energy - enters the Golden Stove of the energy, the energy spot. To do so, you need to empty your mind and stop all thoughts. The correct way of practice is to calm yourself down, clear your mind and sit peacefully as you begin your meditation.   Then, your mental energy will naturally sink down to the Golden Stove with no effort and the process will begin by itself.   Do not try to do it.

One other way to do this is to keep your mind connected with the Medicinal Field, the lower Tan Tien.   Tan Tien is where the energy is produced in the Golden Stove.   You wait for the energy to become strong, then it starts rising.   Then you keep upright, and everything will happen.   Your mind must not use force; your mind needs to be gentle, like before a baby is born.

I would like to give an example of being natural, because people do not know how to be natural anymore.   If, for example, you are pregnant and at 5, 6 or 7 months you try to use strength to start the delivery of the baby, what will happen?   Disaster. Well, you caused that disaster yourself by putting your mind there.   Rather than trying to force things, when the time comes, just let nature take its course, and everything will go smoothly. The baby tells you when it is ready to be born; there is no mistaking the signs of the beginning labor pains.   It is the same in spiritual cultivation: things happen by themselves, whether it be the orbit circulation or the birth of the spiritual baby.

Let us talk a little about the spiritual baby.   Before this can happen, you need to work on the accumulation of the Golden Medicine until it is like a growing fetus.   Orbit circulation needs to start before the spiritual baby begins to grow.   The stage of orbit circulation is for working on internal transportation.

Despite all these long and detailed instructions, orbit circulation is not at all absolutely necessary.   Some people achieve the formation and accumulation of the Golden Immortal Medicine without doing orbit circulation or even without knowing about orbit circulation. In other words, some do it naturally without even being aware of it or knowing about it.

We have not come to the baby yet. There are still other natural ways to achieve the growth of the spiritual baby without doing the orbit circulation. They are hard to describe, thus the ancient achieved ones were forced to set up some guidance for people and taught orbit circulation. If you are smart enough, you just sit in meditation, and everything is achieved by itself. You may even become achieved and not even know about it. I have known many people who achieved themselves and did not even know how it happened. All they did was sit. However, in this moment, it is better that we concentrate on one subject and follow a certain way to achieve a certain purpose. This is all for the beginners.

First you need to gather the energy as true seeds of new life tree or fruit of life inside, so the energy will become strong. Once the energy becomes strong, things happen simply. I will illustrate it with the following example. If there is a thin, gentle flow of water and we dam it up, what happens? The water accumulates. When it is strong enough, it will go where there is a natural channel. Spiritual cultivation is the same. You keep your energy from leaving your body from the channels of your sexual organs (through sex), through your mouth (through too much talking or emotional expression), through your eyes (through watching and reading), etc., and the energy will be dammed up inside your body. You need to wait for that moment when the energy has accumulated and is trying to find a different channel to go through. If your energy is not dammed, and if it has not accumulated in sufficient quantity in the body, it cannot rise up through the body yet.

When the energy rises, there are two main channels in the human body which it uses. The one in the back which runs along the spinal column and over the head is called the general yang energy channel or the Governor Channel. The one in the front which runs up the center of the body is called the general yin energy channel or the Governess Channel. These two channels meet at the mouth. The channels are there already and the energy rises.

Some people who try to force the movement of energy up these channels do not have anything to move because they have scattered their energy through an incorrect lifestyle. Some people try to force it by using their imagination but there is nothing there to move, because they have no energy stored. If there is no dam, there is no accumulated water, so what can be moved? In the case of these people, whether or not it is necessary to dam up the energy is not the question. The question is, why are these people so intent upon forcing things? Do they wish to fly away tomorrow? Many students are like that; they think, "Tonight I will meditate and tomorrow I will fly away." These people are looking for escape. They had best take an honest look at their lives and see what they need to correct or improve first, or they will damage themselves while trying to run away from something.

Once enough energy is gathered, it necessarily has no other place to go than to follow the channel and start circling. It is necessary to allow enough time for accumulation, and then to allow the energy itself to break through whatever obstacle is in its way. This breaking through of obstacles does not happen by the use of your mind, but by the energy itself. The ancient people described feeling the energy meet the blockages and then go through them as follows: "When the pressure of the yin energy (yin pressure here means the body blockage) has been shaken off, it is like the first thunder in the spring, and the body spirit shall be seen."

Q: Master Ni, why do they say shaken off?

Master Ni: It is a strong flow. Sometimes it makes a noise or is something like an earthquake.

It does not matter whether you are a man or a woman, an achieved spirit whose energy has broken through the obstacles or blockages will see light. Yang energy is light. The type of light that is seen depends upon the stage. You first see a small, gentle light, then sometimes you see a yellow, luminous light in a circle that looks like a moon or sometimes like a sun. It is possible to see lights in different colors. Anyway, whether it is a little bit of light or strong light, never be confused by it. This needs real experience.

The light is confusing. Once I thought a moonbeam went through some part of the roof or window, and I tried to feel it. I was silly.

Once the orbit circulation and having seen the light are accomplished naturally and correctly, if you are a person of good virtue, then spiritual beings who know you are a good person will help you. I mean that you do not need to see the spirits. They can contact you directly through various ways. They could be your own body spirits. They notify you what is to be done in the moment; you have foreknowledge. The spirits give you further instruction on the duration of your cultivation. Some teachers also discuss the idea. However, if a teacher has never learned or achieved it, and has no personal experience, that person's words are of no use. The teacher is then just like a parrot saying "Hello, hello," that does not know what the words mean.

The moving energy has certain points - I call them checkpoints, they are also called chakras - to break through in the front and back. These checkpoints are also what I called obstacles before. There are three points in the front, and three points in the back. There are many more points than just those six, but those places are more important than the other ones.

The movement through the checkpoints is done naturally, just as we described the natural movement of the energy. Just because a student knows there are three checkpoints in the back and three checkpoints in the front, it is no use trying to blast your way through a checkpoint like a soldier trying to invade a castle. In other words, I am saying do not try to use your mind to move the energy through the checkpoint. Whatever you can do with your mind is short and temporary; your mind moves away soon. Energy flow is different from the mind moving. It is constant and has real effects over time, just as the stream eventually polishes smooth the surface of a rough rock in its path.

If you move or project your mind, it produces this idea or that. You will think about this and then, in the next moment, think about another thing. If you keep your mind moving, you can make things happen, make a certain spot have feeling, but that is your mind burning the spot. It is not the true energy reaching there. Allow the energy to reach there.

On the back, there are three checkpoints which are yang. They are the point on the tailbone, the middle point between the two shoulder blades and the Jade Pillow, which is the point on the back of the head before the energy then ascends to reach the Mud Pill or Mud Ball. Mud Pill is on the inside of the head, the pivotal point of the brain.

Q: Master Ni, Mud Pill sounds very strange, why do they call it that?

Master Ni: When the true energy, the refined energy reaches here, that part of the brain, which is not a physical organ but a specific location like an acupuncture point, becomes softened like the brain of a baby. Usually the human brain with its internal vessels becomes hardened at different ages according to the conceptions a person holds. It is called "Mud Pill" because it is a small, round location that is pivotal in the sense that it affects the entire brain.

These are the important checkpoints on the energy channel of the back center line.

There are also three yin checkpoints on the front of the body. The yin checkpoints are the Chi Hai (the energy ocean beneath the navel), the Sen Hai (the spiritual ocean on the center of the eyebrows), and the origin of the mind (the Yellow court, which is the place between the nipples). In doing the orbit circulation, the energy itself easily goes through the front three points, because usually there is no obstruction there. The back three points take longer.

When the energy begins to do the orbit circulation, usually the energy will move up the back of the spine, over the head and down the front of the body. That is considered a clockwise movement. If it moves counterclockwise, in the opposite direction, that is okay, but usually it is riskier because the energy flow is reversed. When you need to make the circle movement, the front and back channel all open. Generally, if the energy rises up the front, it will make you pant (fast breathing) and feel short of energy, so it is not recommended. It is better to move it clockwise, although counter-clockwise can be done and is fun, too. Once a person can do one type of circle, he or she can do many types of circles. The movement is natural;

then, you try to move it in different circles in meditation with the purpose of exercising your energy.

Thus, in spiritual cultivation, you use the body as a laboratory or nuclear reactor to produce medicine or power. The medicine produced by the living laboratory someday becomes your new life, and you will be able to move away. This is a result different from just obtaining good health.

What will save you from mortality is a most valuable and simple thing. It is sitting up to watch or feel a very thin line, a line as thin as the thinnest thread, that moves straight up the middle of the spine from the tailbone to the top of the head. That can help you achieve basic health and longevity.

If you force it or belabor it, those main checkpoints or castles will not be conquered. The three checkpoints are the three castles. If you force it, you will not achieve the purpose of spiritual cultivation. So when your energy is not strong enough, you do not need to force anything to move because there is nothing to move. If you use your mind to force the energy to take the castles, that is a big problem. The energy of your mind with desire or expectation is Post-Heaven energy. Any time you force energy with this type of mentality, you make your true energy become gas, like burping. If it becomes gas, it will be scattered in the body and become sickness or give wind or stuffiness. This sickness happens unconsciously to many people, even if they do not do the orbit circulation. Let the energy do its own work. Much of the process happens when you are awake or asleep. If you are not absent-minded or sleeping too deeply, you may be semi-conscious of the internal movement of the energy as it circulates through your body and tries to get through the points.

A general healthy life still produces true energy, but when you become older, the function is also slowly worn out. By true energy I mean the essence of vitality. However, adults do not put the fire under the water, so the energy is not refined. Thus, they do not achieve immortality. Without correct guidance, the true energy will become scattered in a spot, start to stagnate, and then turn out to be of no benefit. Accumulations of things are not healthy in the human body. For example, people who overeat have lots of fat, which becomes deposits in the chin, lower abdomen or side. All of this fat is useless. Some people like this are still healthy, but they are fat. Being too fat surely causes trouble. Similarly, if the energy becomes stagnant in the body, in certain locations, it will become a tumor, a formed lump, cancer or some other trouble in that part of the system where the breakdown of movement has occurred.

Q: If your energy is stagnant or stuck, how do you get it to move?

Master Ni: You can move it. You do not need to worry. Many people naturally live healthy and long lives. The mind should just be corrected so that it moves in the right channel. If a person's mind is not in the right channel, things like emotion will cause stagnation of the energy in certain organs, and then trouble will be caused. For these people, immortality cannot be achieved. The Golden Immortal Medicine produced by internal alchemy or orbit circulation is also called the self-healing power or cure-all medicine. The purpose of internal alchemy is to harmonize the yin and yang energy to produce the self-curing medicine. You produce it inside, and at least you can take care of yourself. However, if you wish alchemy to happen and you force yourself, then you cannot produce the true medicine.

The correct way to do it is first to unite your mind with your body. The center of your body is, as I described, in the navel, so you quietly keep your focus there. If you are a man, when you naturally have an erection you put the fire or mental energy in the Vital Gate. I am not talking about an erection caused by your mind thinking about movie stars or looking at pornography; these things do not bring pure energy. If you are naturally stirred up, before the erection becomes strong, it is the right time to concentrate on the energy and move it to the Medicine Field or lower Tan Tien. If it causes erections to come more often, to come stronger, then you should not wait for the orbit, because it is too strong; the energy has to transform to be general vital force.

This practice of concentrating on the lower Tan Tien will cause you to have erections more often, and they will be stronger. In that case, when the strong erections come, you just directly use the tunnel, the center elevator of the trunk of your body, so the energy does to the crown of the head. It will naturally help the energy transformation and transportation.

This is one way. There are many. Among the many other ways, the simplest is just pure concentration. That will help you.

This instruction of doing the orbit circulation is for men. For women, orbit circulation or gathering the Golden Immortal Medicine is much simpler. Just watch the point between the nipples, slowly and gently. Follow the fourteen details I have given in the book *Mysticism*, but adjust them by yourself. That can help the energy to circulate. Or just simply follow nature, follow Tao, and everything will be done by itself.

X

Now I would like to tell you about the correct time to do this practice. In ancient times, at midnight the ancient achieved ones moved the energy up, and at noon they moved the energy down. Actually, they did not have to move anything, because it happened by the natural cycle of the sun. This practice follows the attraction of the movement of the sun. Let me explain. If the clock is a twenty-four hour cycle, at midnight the sun is below the earth, and at noon the sun is at the top of the sky. In ancient times, a day was divided into 12 energy hours, each energy hour being equivalent to two modern hours. The cycle started at midnight, the bottom, with the rising of the sun from its lowest position. The sun on the top is noontime, which begins the down-slope, the time when the sun starts to sink.

In cultivating oneself, one simply follows the natural cycle of the sun. The most important times for cultivation are the time between midnight and noon, or the time right at noon and the time right at midnight. At noon, the energy is already upward and might be strong, too; it is the time to allow the energy to naturally go downward. I have told you before not to move the energy up at noon because the energy is too strong. This is flexible. It is not good to meditate tightly at noon because the sun has already pulled your internal energy up to the top of your head. Never meditate in the afternoon or evening because that disorders the natural cycle.

The time between midnight and noon is the correct time in the daily cycle for doing the energy movement of orbit circulation. Many people say that meditation can be done at any time.

Yes, you can meditate whenever you feel you can be quiet, but the orbit circulation should be done only in the morning.

The energy in the body travels according to the position of the sun in the sky. At night people have sexual feelings because the energy moves downward and becomes congested in the lower part of the body. In the daytime, the energy is congested in the head area, especially at noontime. In Chinese martial arts, if you hit a certain point on your opponent's head at noon, your opponent will die because the energy is already attracted to the head.

Another way this cycle works is by the year. In the yearly cycle, the first half of the year from the winter solstice to the summer solstice is the upward part of the cycle. When the summer solstice passes, then the downward part of the cycle begins and continues to the winter solstice. This is the orbit of the earth around the sun.

Q: Master Ni, how does the yearly orbit relate to one's personal meditation?

Master Ni: Do the opposite activities from where the energy is naturally located. In the summer, when the sun attracts the energy to my head, I would keep my energy low or, ideally, inactive. Whatever the conditions, still continue to engage in all kinds of life activity. A couple, for example, might engage in occasional sex during the hot summer months. In winter, I do the opposite, which is read and study to keep the energy in my head. This is the ideal standard; of course, each person needs to make adjustments to fit his or her life situation.

This is the whole thing called orbit circulation. Orbit circulation is not a coined term. It is the natural cycle which produces the physical reaction with the human body, because human beings are children of the sun. Practically, if you gently concentrate and let the sun naturally do the job, you do not create any stagnation and you live long with no problem. The daily movement of the sun through the sky was observed by the ancient achieved ones. They did not have a way to train or discipline their students, so they moved that sun cycle to the body to illustrate the natural energy circulation as the orbit energy circulation of spiritual cultivation.

Achieved practitioners of the Integral Way sometimes describe it another way, saying that in the morning, the yang energy is strong and the yin energy is weak. In the afternoon, the yin energy is strong and yang energy is weak. You do not need to disorder it; disordering it brings no benefit. If you live naturally, you can let the sun do the job. What is your part? You have only two things to do: First, in the early morning, welcome the sun. This is why at midnight you automatically wake up. When you wake up, sit a little while, such as ten minutes or more, then go back to sleep. Second, at night you feel sleepy, so go to sleep. Let the descending of the energy fulfill itself naturally. Do not cause any unnatural imbalance. In the morning, the energy itself goes up, why make it go down? In the evening, the energy naturally goes down, why make it go up?

There is a correct time to sit in meditation. In the early morning, you do it, especially after midnight. If you do it at that time, you can see more effect. Traditionally, the most effective time to meditate is the meeting point of yin energy and yang energy; that time is the first energy hour of the daily cycle, which is midnight.

Q: About meditation, every day my meditation is different. I do not think I am an excellent meditator. However, sometimes at random times during the day, but especially when I have been quietly working at my desk for a while in the afternoon, I feel a vibration or shaking inside, not in the back or front, but in the middle. It goes up to about the middle of my chest and it stops. Is that anything that you are talking about?

Master Ni: We should not discuss individual symptoms here. Too many people have different symptoms. I only give general instruction.

Something else we need to talk about is how strong the mind should be when you do the orbit circulation. We are supposed to use the mind only when the energy flows down to have sexy feeling. When that happens, use the mind to pull the energy back up. In general, let the energy flow happen naturally. With a strong mind, it is easy to make the energy move, but it is hard to make the energy move gently. If your mind is too gentle, then you become scattered.

This becomes an important point of spiritual cultivation. The first thing to learn in spiritual cultivation is how to restore the naturalness of the mind. We are unnatural, because we continually use our minds to keep thinking about things. We keep thinking about things that are already past or have not happened yet. We still keep thinking. Every day we use the mind busily to do this and do that, so we have already lost our naturalness.

In spiritual cultivation, you need first to discipline the monkey mind. Then you need to restrain the wild horse of your intent. If somebody's mind or yang fire is too strong, it will not be helpful to the body. This will sometimes cause congestion of the blood in certain areas like the head or the lower abdomen. This needs to be noticed and corrected if necessary. The wild intent is what keeps us overly involved in worldly things, being impulsive, etc.

XI

Above, I am talking about the big principles of spiritual cultivation. Because Chinese spiritual practice has become so confused, and there are so many schools, I feel the basic guidelines are important. There are some real achieved teachers, but quite often they teach only for the purpose of making money, or just for social promotion, but quite often there is no reality to their achievement. This is why I am not attached to any specific school, but just give the basic reality of this traditional practice. There are lots of questions from the people who practice such things. If they learn naturalness, usually it is safe.

I would like to mention something. If the energy is too low, then there are lots of feelings of desire for sex. This may cause internal pressure and make you wish to do something. If the energy is too high, it will cause you to become nervous and fearful, but you cannot do anything about what is to happen and about being nervous. The best principle is centeredness; not too high, not too low, but safe.

Q: Master Ni, if a person is too high or too low as you described, how does he or she return to centeredness?

Master Ni: Use mental conducting to guide the energy to be centered by pulling the energy away and focusing on the Yellow Altar, the middle point between the two nipples.

The achievement of immortality depends upon how deeply you know the naturalness of nature and of life. If you learn naturalness, immortality is not far. It is not an illusion or fantasy. It is closer than your hand.

Q: When the circulation begins, what does it feel like?

Master Ni: When doing the orbit circulation, you may feel a slight warmth in the section of the channel where the energy moves through. A cold feeling is not healthy. The feeling of warmth is still not important. Yes, you feel it and you know about it, but the movement of energy is important, not the feeling of the movement of energy. You know, every day you have energy circulation; it happens naturally, but you do not notice it. Because you do not notice it, it is normal. If you notice it, it is not normal, it has become much stronger. Some people become crazy about it; they would like to feel it. To somebody who likes to know about spiritual reality, I would give the reality, and I talk about the unity of spiritual reality and the material foundation of the body. You feel the warmth, you see the light, you hear the voice, you feel the energy shocks (the little twitches) - that is physical reality, and it is also spiritual reality. In the spiritual realm, you see the same one deep reality. There is a unified world in depth. Feeling the movement of the energy is not important; the movement is important.

Q: How do you know if you are doing it, if you cannot feel it?

Master Ni: You do it by your visual energy work internally. This is the key point.

The purpose of doing orbit circulation or energy movement is twofold: one purpose is to sublimate your sexual energy, which means to move the sexual energy away so you achieve health and longevity. The other purpose is to refine the Immortal Medicine, then you become yang spiritual energy. Yang spiritual energy stays with the body and once your physical body fails, it brings survival.

Q: If you have an energy leak, then you could not do this, right?

Master Ni: If you have an energy leak, you rest a few days and restore your energy again.

Q: So then you have to build up the energy like a dam, or else it dissipates?

Master Ni: There are two ways to do this. One way is to build the foundation for a hundred days. During this one hundred days of building the foundation, you should not have sex. If you want to feel the energy moving, doing the one hundred days is the way to do it. After one hundred days, some people still do some sexual practice for adjustment, but other people still continue to be celibate. That is one way.

Q: You said you have to build up your energy.

Master Ni: In general, after you lay down the foundation, you can still have a sexual life. There is an ancient term for it: "Before, three; afterward, four." This means before you have sex, stop doing your cultivation for three days, and after you have sex, do not resume your cultivation for four days. Then you start to do meditation again. Spiritual people, more or less, would like to follow this principle, although this is harder for everyone to follow exactly. This is why there are lots of festivals, lots of birthdays of this divinity and that divinity, all invented to make general people decrease their sexual life. That is the ancient spiritual promotion. Spiritual teachers designed these festivals for general people, so that on certain days they could do it and on certain other days, they could not do it. Energywise, the instruction is: no cultivation for three days before sex and for four days after; then you start meditation again.

A hundred days was specifically designed for this purpose of building the foundation. It is an organized way to do it.

At last, I would like to conclude that the energy circulation in our body is a natural function. In this chapter, we discuss the orbit circulation. It is one type of energy circulation which is commanded by the mind, but it is to enhance the natural function of energy circulation of the body, it is what we learn from nature to enhance energy circulation. It must be done naturally with some amount of development. It cannot be done unnaturally, otherwise how can it be what we learned from nature?

It is natural for a person of energy cultivation - who does not overwork during the day - to wake up at midnight and find one's sexual energy stirred up. Before it becomes too strong and becomes sexual fluid, you can take this energy and transform it to be your own tonic. In other words, before the chi type of energy transforms to become the watery type of energy, the possibility exists of transporting this energy back to the center of the head.

You know, the root of a tree is on the bottom, but the root of human people is on their head. Sexual energy stirred up by the stimulation of the eyes is from above. Then, you generate the sexual organ to accommodate the sexual energy that comes from the kidneys or perineum and other parts of the body to be transformed into sexual fluid to let it go. Before the erection becomes too strong, before this bit of energy, chi, transforms itself into sexual fluid, if you are aware of the bodily energy circulation, you immediately stop it and guide the energy back to the center of the body or the head. This something, this energy, before it is transformed into sexual fluid, is called medicine or Golden Immortal Medicine by achieved cultivators.

Spiritually achieved individuals are ambitious to manage their own life without allowing the lower physical nature to steal their energy and hasten their death. This is how the orbit circulation was established as a general practice. At the beginning, it was just an idea. Sometime later, the achieved teachers needed to teach their students and so made it into a formal practice. I would like to tell you the truth: the orbit circulation as artificial movement is not necessary. The only thing necessary to do is to stop the chi from becoming sexual fluid. This is done by naturally waking up and sitting for a few minutes so that the energy moves up into the head. Waking up itself is the rising or attraction of the energy to come back to the head. If at the time you wake up, you do some meditation, a few Dao-In exercises, or do nothing, just stay awake for a short while, the energy leak will be stopped. And what you have done is gather what is called Immortal Medicine. By accumulating

Immortal Medicine night after night, you naturally become stronger and all organs have and enjoy the richness of energy support within. This is why it is called Immortal Medicine.

The second step in immortal practice which comes after a certain amount of the Golden Immortal Medicine has been accumulated is to form the spiritual baby, which is the light you see in the darkness of night. If you are too tight or too tense, this subtle light cannot grow because of suffocation from the mind. If you allow it to go out when the baby is not strong enough, then it will disappear in the natural surroundings. Therefore, there is some instruction about how to proceed with the spiritual evolution when you come to this stage.

When most people see the white light, they call it an angel, Quan Yin, the White Brother, the warrior who holds the sword riding on the white horse, etc. The reality is that this is still only the surface of the deep spiritual reality. The deep spiritual reality is Tao. When most people see golden light, they call it Buddha or God. They do not know that these visions are still only the offspring of their own spiritual reality; they are not external to one's own self.

Before reaching this stage, the general study I offer in my books is quite enough, more than enough. Few people come to this stage, and when you do, then you need a spiritual teacher. The foundation, the good instruction for being able to reach this stage, has been given in all my works. The orbit circulation, the mental ability to route one's chi around the skin of your body, can also be achieved. However, the greatest value of this practice is mostly the part where the chi is guided from the lower part of the body through the spine to the head. The spinal cord is the center of the nervous system. Through meditation, T'ai Chi Movement and Dao-In, you can achieve this purpose of bringing the energy to the head.

However, you must know that when this happens, you become sensitive. The degree or condition of your sensitivity becomes almost too acute. This also brings disbenefit. For example, when I was young, I could drink cold beer; one cup or a little more was no problem at all. However, after you really open the channel from the bottom to the top, the alcohol content of beer, even only a half cup, can knock you out - it makes you unconscious. I mean it makes me pass out, because the transportation of vaporizing alcohol to the center of the head happens so fast.

XII

The last suggestion I offer you is how to use this information I am giving. When you do spiritual self-cultivation, it is not suitable to be too tight. If you are too tight, your practice will be unnatural. The practice we do is just to develop nature a little more for our own benefit. I suggest to all my friends to just remember the principles we discussed in this material. Most important are the big principles. You have to do them right. During your cultivation and meditation, do not be crazy about the different sensations or different experiences, or small symptoms. Do not think too much about them unless they are negative. You know that they are negative when it does not help you to achieve your purpose. If it is negative, stop doing it and restore your general, ordinary life.

At first, pay attention to the big guidance. The small details will be naturally fulfilled in the stage of realization.

There are several types of spiritual practices. Some are more apparent and easier to learn. Some are more subtle and hard to control. There are different practices and instruction for all ages of people.

I recommend that young students (up to 30 or 40) set their goal as being 75% on the pursuit of wisdom and enlightenment, 25% on specific practices. By wisdom I mean accumulating sufficient knowledge from reading, listening to people who do well in life, and your own observation of how things happen in the world to make a safe place for your life and a safe place in the world for all people. You also work toward having some kind of financial stability. Wisdom also means reading sufficient spiritual books to become familiar with the terminology. By enlightenment I mean actually applying knowledge and wisdom which you have obtained through reading, etc. and using it to improve your life and surroundings and attain Unobstructed Vision, which means learning to see what things or situations really are, not just what they look like superficially. I also recommend that young students learn practices such as Dao-In, T'ai Chi exercise and Chi Kung (Chi Gong), etc. It is also suitable to learn a little bit about meditation, which involves coming to understand your mind. You will see no good result in your meditation before you understand everything, so do not expect quick results. As you grow more and more, you know the pursuit of wisdom and enlightenment can offer you as much as your life scope can develop.

In the next stage, you become older and more mature, so I suggest setting your goal to be 50% on wisdom and enlightenment and 50% on specific practices.

After turning 50, 60 or 70, you become much more mature. The pursuit of wisdom and enlightenment at this stage might perhaps only take 25% of your attention, and you might put the other 75% into your practice and realistic cultivation. At that stage, you need more cultivation to support your internal energy. For example, women, when they are young, do not need a lot of cosmetics. They still look nice and beautiful to me. They also do not need lots of beautiful dresses; they naturally look fresh and attractive. After their middle years, women need to pay more attention to how they look, because they were naturally good looking when they were young. The same is true for men. For both men and women, spiritual practice is of tremendous importance. The internal spiritual energy cultivation will make their beauty and life enduring and maintain their youthful look. Although being good looking is an external thing, if you give up your external things, what is your internal reality? Both are important.

These percentages I give are just general guidelines which apply to both women and men. This is a lifetime learning, it cannot be done quickly. Of course, there will be individual variation because people's lives are different according to their family situation, etc. It is important to read and study, and it is important to do the practices, if a person truly wants to understand and make progress.

Whether or not a person achieves himself or herself in this life, every effort you make moves you in the right direction of making progress for the future. Thus, if you feel that it is too late for you, or you cannot gather enough energy because of your health condition or life situation, do not feel frustrated or defeated. Use the strength of your study and mental energy to plant an inner willingness to be open to internal teachings that will keep you moving in the correct spiritual direction to maxi-mize present or future growth.

Wisdom, mental clarity and spiritual purity are needed in every age of your life. Nobody can be excused from not becoming improved internally, spiritually, mentally and emotionally. When you use this information, you need to look at your stage to decide how seriously you will do the practice. In general, do not put yourself together in a single 'investment.' If you do, there is still specific instruction to learn from some experienced achieved ones. This is also important to know when you engage in special cultivation.

However, I give all the important instructions at various levels. Your development and serious study are necessary to make all the knowledge become part of your life.

Chapter 5

The Unity
between Metaphysics and Physics,
Nature and Society

The spiritual trend of pioneer spiritually achieved ones is to explore the depths of how the world and life came into being. They do not presume what existed before the world. This allows their spiritual development to bring about their own understanding of the truth of immortality. Master Chen Tuan was one of those who kept making such an effort. In this chapter, I would like to present what has been achieved by masters of different generations who found their own confidence to live a natural life harmoniously with universal nature itself.

Natural spiritual truth is indefinable. If it is defined, it can be defined only in one way or another because language is linear. However, spiritual truth is all the ways and directions. If the integral truth cannot be defined, then how do we learn it? We might discuss it. Through discussion, we may reach somewhere. However, talk and ideas are different from assertively trying to define spiritual reality.

Some ancient teachers decided that natural spiritual energy has two levels. The deepest level is totally beyond all conceptual effort. The more superficial level can be discussed. Thus, in order to serve the conceptual mind, the subtle truth can be discussed with beginners.

1. The Spiritual Truth Is the Universal Fertile Energy
Universal energy is the universal law. It prevails in everything and every being as the universal subtle reality. It is the common source of all, including material and spiritual reality.

A. How the Universe Was Formed
Before the formation of the physical universe, the prime substance, which later developed into the physical universe, existed. Yet, it could not be seen or heard. Spiritual energy depends upon no external force. It has no form and no

sound, yet it reaches everywhere. It continues to generate as the fountain of all things, embracing all things and, at the same time, prevailing within them.

B. The Universe Is Formed of Energy

First, the subtle origin gave birth to the primal or spiritual energy. The primal energy is the indistinguishable existence. We say it is indistinguishable because it is unified into one and has no separation or form. Then, the primal energy extended itself by its own movement or self-operation. Two energy phases were recognized as yang - or impetus - and yin - inertia or resistance. These two types of energy began to interplay and a third, mild energy was produced. The different combinations of the basic three produced all things. What is the name of the third energy? It has no name, but it is all lives which are the combination of the first two types of energy, yin and yang.

C. The Subtle Origin Remains Independent of Its Creations

Although the Subtle Origin produces everything, it remains independent from all things that it produces. The Subtle Spiritual Energy is different from all concrete things or ideas, so it remains unnameable and inconceivable. All nameable and conceivable things were begotten by the unnameable, inconceivable Subtle Truth.

D. Change Is the Constancy of the Universe

No object or thing at the definable, conceivable level lasts forever. On that level, there is a permanent flow of changes from nonbeing to being and from being to nonbeing. This is the constancy of the universe. The law that causes things to change is also called Spiritual Law. Life, creativity and continuity harmonize with Spiritual Reality. Death, destruction and mutation or sudden variation are in disharmony with Spiritual Reality.

E. The Relationship Between the Things

All things at the definable, conceivable level are interdependent. Nothing gives birth to something. Something gives birth to nothing. Sometimes things confront each other, but simultaneously on a different level, those things are also unified. No position is fixed; things shift back and forth into different positions.

Conflict is unavoidable. When confrontation becomes radical, destruction occurs. When confrontation between positions shifts smoothly, Subtle Harmony is reached. A smooth shift from confrontation to unification is possible. This is what brings new opportunity. A smooth shift in human life means wise concession.

F. The Masterly Energy of the Universe

In the universe, there is no supreme master who has a will and who has emotional reactions of preference, anger, sadness and happiness. Nor is there any supreme master who is lord over the world of gods or over nature and human beings. There is only the Subtle Law. Thus, you do not need to fear that there is a God who will punish you, you only need to fear that you yourself will engage in doing things that are against the Subtle Law.

The sky is part of universal nature. Its nature is similar to that of the subtle law. It has no will, and it gives no reward to good and no punishment to bad. The sky is not directly capable of dominating other beings nor can it interfere with the will of other beings. The sky is only one of all things.

If a God exists, in the common Western concept of a kind or stern man who lives in the sky, he must be some thing. If he lives on the level of things, he must die like all things. However, God is not a thing; God is an energy. God is not the Subtle Origin, which is beyond your conception.

G. Cultural Creations through the Expression of Philosophy and Religions Can Deviate from Nature

Philosophers used the four elements of water, fire, air and earth to describe the source of the world. Sometimes they used the eight terms sky, earth, water, fire, wind, thunder, mountain and lake, or other systems to generalize and describe different aspects of nature. These systems of description were attempts to use nature to describe nature.

They did not relate much to religious worship, which was an attempt to know; they only touched the superficial or external structure of nature, even though they were talking about energies instead of matter.

Similarly, in other systems or ways of understanding life, philosophers attempted to use a part to explain the whole, or to use simple matters to explain the general. They all failed of necessity. The part cannot tell the whole; the simple element cannot tell the entirety. Tao, as the integral truth, is above all.

H. Creative Energy Is Also Called Natural Impetus

The natural impetus is to be and to do. Natural impetus leads to evolution. It is the nature of the process of evolution for things to become better and stronger. The projection of the impetus of nature can be expressed in different stages and levels.

Natural impetus could miss its creative target by emitting energy that is either too low or too high, too much or too little. Extremes bring about mistakes. Also, creativity which pushes too hard produces negativity or resistance.

I. Subtle Law Reveals Itself on the Level of Yin and Yang

The subtle law expresses the unity and harmony which surpasses all differences and conflicts of relative phenomena. Relative phenomena are paired opposites such as big and small, not enough and too much, high and low, far and near, light and heavy, white and black, cold and hot, life and death, restful and restless, beautiful and ugly, good and bad, strong and weak, trouble and blessing, honor and disgrace, good luck and misfortune, right and wrong, superior and inferior, poor and rich, orderly and disorderly, skillful and clumsy, true and false, public and private, etc. These pairs all oppose each other and at the same time establish each other. Conceptually or in reality, they are interdependent and co-existent. This expresses universal objectivity.

When they are in a normal range, the opposites serve each other by competing with each other or with other similar pairs. This brings about constant forwardness and progress in development.

J. Extreme Yin Turns into Yang, and Vice Versa

The most important message in this chapter is that an extreme extension in any one single direction leading to lack of balance will bring about the opposite destination. For example, people may not like hard work or a hard life, but the right amount of hard work and a hard life make people strong. People prefer leisure and enjoyment, but an overdose of leisure and enjoyment weakens people's physical systems, etc. Therefore, balance is important.

2. Life Is Nothing More than Energy

Human life comes from universal energy. Universal energy is complete in individual human life just as it is in nature or universal life. Universal life contains both spiritual and physical energies. When human life develops a complete mentality, it becomes almost equal to nature itself. Human life is a concentrated example of universal life.

Because human life is a small model of the universe, humans can love one another in order to fulfill the function of innate universal energy. When energy converges, a life form is shaped. When energy disperses, a life form is dissolved.

There is something in the circumstance of living you call self. However, there is no self in an individual sense, only the universal self which continues to transform itself in all lives.

If you live at the lower end of the great life, you serve others as a tool of universal nature. If you live at the high end of the great life, you embrace all lives as yourself. This is called boundless universal life. Boundless universal life is realized by boundless universal love.

A. Energy Always Moves and Flows - Do Nothing to Stop Its Movement

On the surface, all the things of the world are like the water flowing in a river which moves and changes unceasingly. There is conflict in all changes. If you see conflict, you see duality. To lift yourself from duality is to follow the way of unity, harmony and balance. It is the result of dissolving new conflict. It is not stagnancy. One cannot find unity, harmony and balance where there are no changes.

By being centered, not taking sides and not being partial, nothing is overly done and nothing is under done. Constant normalcy produces a clear way which can be easily followed. Therefore, all extremes need to be avoided. To do so, make no groundless assumptions or assertions, and do not be stubborn or self-opinionated. Self-opinionated here means to be obstinate in holding to one's opinion or view, etc. It is related to having opinions about things based upon one's past experiences.

All things are in the process of development. With certain conditions, balance is maintained while development takes place. Balance leads to progress. Imbalanced development leads to extremity and the loss of poise.

B. Social Order Follows the Flow of Natural Rhythm

A social order must not be established by force, but by correct understanding of the direction toward which people are willing to move.

A correct social order is maintained by people with a sense of honor. Most people like to be honored. This is a reliable tendency of people. People may do something bad in private, but normally they will not humiliate themselves in public. Because sometimes people make mistakes, they invent ideologies to cover their improper behavior. However, behavior done with wrong intention or bad motives is more serious; it leads to spiritual downfall.

C. Circumstances Cause People to Look Other Than Good

In the normal range of life activities, people do not display anything good or bad. They look neutral but move toward good. Good and bad are expressions of life situations which have been influenced by circumstances. Moving toward good is the destination of the nature of human life.

In its depth, pristine human nature is the same as the nature of the universe, which is positive and tends toward good, truth and beauty. In normal circumstances, we trust people because the pure human nature, before becoming damaged or twisted, is good. By following the pure goodness, truth and beauty of one's untwisted pristine nature, one can avoid being entrapped by circumstances in the stage of post-Heaven or worldly life. When one is not entrapped by circumstance, one can restore one's own spiritual purity.

Everybody participates in circumstances. Being entrapped means being pulled down by those circumstances and being unable to maintain one's balance. Not being entrapped means being able to do just fine, whatever your circumstances, or arranging your circumstances to maximize your existence in the world.

D. Universal Nature Manifests as Love

The core of human nature is humanistic love. You love, so you live. You live for love. At least you love your life. This is universal humanistic nature. However, if you only love your own life, you do not love other lives. This happens if you have not looked deeply into self-nature, which contains the entirety of human society. To love only oneself is to live a partial, incomplete life. It is a pity to live a partiality and not live the wholeness of life. If you do not live the wholeness of life, you waste the life opportunity.

The life-loving human spirit needs to be nurtured in everyday practice. By nurturing the human spirit, one becomes courageous, righteous, powerful and immortal and unites with universal nature. One has no fear in life.

E. Awakened Spiritual Energy Produces Intuitive or Internal Knowledge

Internal knowledge brings feelings of sympathy and shame. This happens because when you begin to be aware of what is inside yourself, you find everything, not just the positive spiritual qualities of universal love and wisdom, but you also meet your conscience and sense of individuality. Internal knowledge also brings understanding of when one is being unreasonable and needs to make a concession. Internal knowledge brings the understanding of when it is best to decline a persuasive offer that only brings benefit to oneself. Internal knowledge knows when you are wrong and need to make a change.

Thus, internal knowledge is moral knowledge that protects oneself as well as other people. The achievement of internal knowledge is expressed even among primitive people. A good civilization develops the useful spiritual awareness of internal knowledge. This spiritual awareness can only be sufficiently developed when the core of human nature - that is, humanistic love - is well nurtured and protected from bad influences in one's living situation. Intellectual study can also help one to rediscover and realize the core of human nature.

F. Civilization Can Be a Manifestation of Universal Nature

The core of human nature is the core of universal nature, from which the birth of life was a necessary development. From the core of human nature, the high quality of human civilization developed. Thus, whatever you do against the trend of human civilization goes against human nature and deeper universal nature. This core of human life has no need of religious decoration or labeling.

3.   The Subtle Law Is the Truth

All things are subject to change. The only thing that is not subject to change is the subtle law; it exists as a part of all changes. The subtle law does not exist separately from the changes of all things.

People take concepts for the truth. They do not see that concepts exist only in the relative sphere. Truth is not a concept, it is what exists behind concepts. Nor do people realize that others do not necessarily understand the conceptual truth that they hold, because everybody has different life experiences and therefore different concepts.

Unified or absolute truth is not conceptual. That is because it is in everything. There is no single concept which can serve all people during all times and all circumstances as the ultimate truth. The wise choose not to conceptualize the truth. The wise allow the truth to be the truth, but the minds of ordinary people always attempt to describe the truth in their own way, which comes from their limited experience or development. Their partial way harms others and harms themselves.

A. The Only Safe Standard Is, "Is That Natural?"
Truth can be interpreted as a standard which determines wrong or right. However, no standard can be established that will serve all times and all people. Standards are always relative to some place, some society and a certain time. Standards only describe a common element in a collection of conditions. Standards are subject to change when the time, place and fashion in society changes. Standards change when the conditions that built them change.

A free society allows many standards; in other words, it allows differences. Rigid institutions such as certain branches of the Catholic church or the communist party allow only one standard for all people. They call it an objective standard, but it is not objective because it is ill-adapted to the needs of the people it is supposed to regulate. A so-called objective standard which is applied to judge what is right or wrong does not exist.

The only true objective standard that can be applied to human life is whether or not something is natural. Someone can explain any standard (including being natural) or promote it, but not impose it on other people. If they impose it upon someone, it is not the absolute objective standard of truth any more. This is the simplest fact that can be twisted by priests and communist intellectuals. One can know the true standard from its opposite, the false standards.

B. Your True Being Is Not What You Experience
A human being consists of multiple beings in one individual being. These are the physical being, emotional being, mental being and spiritual being. When one's being extends to the external sphere, there is the health being, intellectual being, social being and financial being, all of which assist your life. In the world, people typically judge others by their external beings rather than by their internal beings. Typically, people build themselves by working on

their external being and neglect the true foundation, the internal being.

What is your true being? According to people's level of maturity, the answer will be different.

In spiritual teaching, the true being has no self. The sense of self is an idea that is supported by receiving input from the external environment. If you contemplate the world and yourself, you will find that there is no separation between yourself and the external environment. For example, you cannot live in this world without having provisions, a physical body and a certain amount of intellectual knowledge. These are the conditions of a life on earth. In addition, you depend upon all life conditions to support your life. These conditions, however, are not your true being or true self.

Then, what is your true being or true self? Your true being is anything that cannot be produced or reduced.

Are the conditions that support your life still the same as they were in the past? Some conditions would be the same and some would be different. That which does not change is your true being.

Will the conditions that support your life be the same in the future as they are now? The answer is the same as the answer about the past. Some conditions will be the same, and some other things will be different.

Thus, we know that the external conditions of the past, present and future all change. Therefore, the true being lives with the most essential and allows what would change to change. That which is most essential is called the True Being; this is what the achieved ones respect. Spiritual teaching says, the true being is non-being, the true self is no self. When you break the boundary of beingness and the self, then you reach spiritual truth.

C. The Spirit and the Mind Make Good Partners

The function of the mind is to know what is good and what is bad. The value of this knowledge, however, does not stop at purely knowing about it. The value of knowledge is the application. That is what is most helpful to a person's life.

When something is good, go forward, and when something is bad, retreat. There is advantage and benefit in good, and there is trouble and harm in bad.

Spiritually, you are taught to be equal-minded, which means to have a non-discriminating mind. This is spiritual cultivation, however, not worldly living. The correct term is "having an equal-minded and non-discriminative spirit that lets your mind serve your life correctly." In practical life, you cannot be equal-minded; you cannot accept a con artist who has a disguised evil plan and treat that person the same as you would treat your benefactor. Knowing what is good and bad, and responding to things accordingly, is letting your mind serve your life correctly.

Spiritual teaching is meant to serve the high part of one's life and helps to lift the low part. It is wise to let spiritual education serve one's essential life. It is unwise to misapply spiritual education to replace or to block the good function of the mind.

Spiritual education and the mind serve a human life on two different levels. For an effective life, it is important that the two harmonize with each other rather than have one dominate the other. Harmony and balance between spiritual education and mind are important.

When one meets a situation of uncertainty, the mind needs to give some time for the spirit to function, for example, overnight. If you do not receive a spiritual message overnight, still do not let the mind become assertive, but wait until the spiritual message is received.

When there is no uncertainty, practice maintaining an equal and non-discriminative mind. This will help you keep your balance. However, the spiritual quality of the people you deal with cannot be neglected. In other words, you must protect yourself when necessary. This is a key to protecting one's health and peace of mind.

A good spirit supports a good mind and a good mind supports a good spirit. The body is the foundation of both the spirit and the mind.

Rigid teaching would harm the user of the teaching. In other words, learn widely.

D. The Pursuit of Social Fashions Could Be a Trap

Freedom is the essence of healthy living. Self-respect is the mother of freedom. People who have spiritual self-respect do not accept or help build any social type of religious control. People who have a sense of self-respect do not accept or help build a slavery system, nor do they support the ruling of a maniac or control of political gangsters as in the communist system.

Because people do not know what will happen if they accept or give help to a new religious or political or social fashion, they exchange their self-respect cheaply for a new fashion. Once a social fashion is formed, most people suffer trouble. People are only awakened to the trouble after the force of custom has already been established. Then it takes a lot of effort to undo it because of those who are still attached to the custom, believing it to be something most valuable and meaningful.

Once a social fashion has become a custom, it generates great force and strength. Many people think it is valuable and meaningful and become attached to it. However, when others understand the trouble that social fashion causes, they know that it takes a lot of trouble to undo or change it.

Let us take the historical Catholic church and communist rule as examples of social fashion. They started as a fashion, and were built with the help of many people. However, unconsciously, they have sold out; the freedom of the soul is ignored. They have traded their self-respect for a type of slavery.

The early achieved ones warned about this kind of trouble over 2,500 years ago. The early spiritual people based their knowledge on the natural foundation of life. They respected living with individual spiritual nature rather than bending to any external force, whether it be a political, religious or social establishment. Exchanging what is true for what is untrue is the downfall of human spiritual life. It brings devolution and undevelopment.

The positive message here is that by being content with one's spiritual nature, one can enjoy the spiritual freedom that is priceless. Be wise and do not trade your priceless freedom for the priced freedom. The priced freedom creates a certain type of lifestyle. It creates a comfortable place to live, ability to purchase enjoyments, interest in doing what will bring about excitement, highly priced luxuries, social vanity and glory and a lot of flatterers who can satisfy your swollen psychology. If you have no choice other than to live within a religion or in a restricted or communist society, you can still maintain your spiritual freedom.

To learn integral spiritual truth is to learn a reasonable, balanced way of wise life management with spiritual development at its center.

4.   Desire Is the Foundation of Life, but Sublimation Serves Profoundly

People have desire. Life is expressed by its desire. The reality of life is a continual process of issuing and fulfilling desires. This is, however, a half-lived life. The other half of life is elimination of less important desires, finding a better way to fulfill the important desires, and having respect and knowledge for the things that are not based on desire. This way of life includes not only taking, but also giving.

In barbaric societies, there is only one element: desire. In a civilized society, there are two elements: desire and civilization that modifies and decorates desires. In spiritual individuals and communities, desires are not fulfilled, but sublimated. This brings about wisdom and spiritual development.

A. Self-Respect Is the Foundation of a Good Society or Government

Self-respect is a privilege of developed societies which distinguishes them from the slave societies of ancient and modern times. A slave society is one in which all individuals are subject to the tyrannical control of the government.

If the laws of a country are established to protect the authority of the government rather than to serve the people, they are evil. Law should be rooted in the self-respect of the people. The self-respect of all individuals produces mutual respect among people. From mutual respect, mutual agreement on a contract or law will produce a suitable effect.

The universal subtle law is the supreme law among all things and all beings. It is spiritual wisdom that the subtle law is the mother of all good laws. A principle is produced by wisdom like "Do not do unto people what you do not like people to do unto you." An immature student revised it as "Do unto people what you would like people to do unto you," the so-called "golden rule" familiar to many in the West. This revised version encouraged interference, interruption and bothering. This revised version creates the expectation of favors from other people, loss of self-respect and loss of self-reliance.

B. The Cyclical Pattern of Nature Can Be Your Important Knowledge

We can trust the constancy of nature. We can trust the cyclic pattern of nature. The rhythmic movements of nature's cycles can produce recognition of the existence of the subtle law. Some primitive people thought that someone operated the cycle; thus, they produced the concept of a powerful God.

Because the constancy of nature offers the security of the big life of the universe, the cycle is nature itself. There is no need for an external operator. The concept of an external operator was primitive. Once the understanding of an external operator has dissolved, trust in the will of God is also non-existent.

The powerful movement of nature expresses the subtle law of constancy. When a person knows and accepts the subtle law that moves all things and all existence, a person can maintain a certain amount of control over the internal and external forces of one's own life.

Generally, there are two ways to control nature; one way is to manage nature according to the laws of nature. Another way is to manage nature by ignoring it. Different results will be brought about by each approach. The former achieves a good life through using nature and is the way of the spiritually developed person. The latter disturbs and harms the organic condition of nature and is followed by the person who has not yet learned deeply about himself or herself.

C. The Integral Truth Is Hun Tun, the Gate of All Wonders (Miracles)

At the beginning of the universe existed the primal energy, which is also called Hun Tun. Hun Tun is undefinable. Later, Hun Tun became a special term to describe a stage of universal growth that is undefinable. If it were definable, it would be not called Hun Tun.

From Hun Tun, two types of energy developed: yang or light energy, and yin or heavy energy. Yang energy permeates everything and transforms itself when it is in a specific environment. It is also called Heavenly energy because of its activeness and constancy in moving and making changes. Yin energy condenses itself into form. It is also called earthly energy because of its density and physical form.

From the interplay of yang and yin, the multiplicity of things and beings are born. From the multiplicity in the world, yang and yin are recognized. Yin reacts to yang. Yin is produced by yang when yang extends itself to the extreme of being too active. Then a new stage develops, starting with activity but eventually becoming stagnant. When yin extends itself to extreme inactivity or stagnancy, it dissolves back to be moving energy again. Yin also expresses a stage of life that cannot maintain itself as formed energy any more, but continues to sink and deteriorate.

Thus, yang and yin are not absolute. They are the basic relative pattern of the universe that only exists in the secondary level of the phenomenal world. When we trace back to the origin of yang and yin, the oneness of Hun Tun is there. Hun Tun functions as the subtle gate through which energy enters and exits, participating in self-transformation from non-beingness to beingness and vice versa, from nothingness to somethingness and vice versa, from manifested objects to non-manifested essence and vice versa. This subtle gate is Hun Tun. Hun Tun is the Integral Truth. The Integral Truth is undefinable reality.

D. Cultivate to Move to the Balance of Becoming Materialized and Spiritualized

To cultivate oneself spiritually is to cultivate one's own life energy. To cultivate spiritually is to swim in the subtle way where a person does not come or go. Spiritual energy moves and exercises in the central way. There the Integral Way becomes a path for things to come and go and for things to move between the two extremes. The Subtle Spiritual Origin maintains itself in peace, enjoyment, freedom and eternity. That is where Heaven is forming and where the immortals, gods and goddesses live.

To those who know to center themselves, Hun Tun is the eternal energy of the universe. All things swell in the energy flow and continue their transformation. All things stay in the flow; nothing can stop. That is the path - that is spiritual truth. Spiritual truth is ever-lasting.

However, spiritual integration does not last on the edge, it lasts in the center. Movement, flow and transformation happen to external things which are on the edge. At the center of all things, there is something unchangeable which stays on the chi level.

When a life's yang and yin energy embrace each other, that life is maintained. When the two energies separate and part, death happens. As long as the form (yin) of life holds the energy (yang) of life, life keeps going on.

To learn natural spiritual truth is to know to embrace yang energy and enhance the substance of the universal life force by embracing the potency of Hun Tun. When chi becomes strong, and a person's sharp vision is functioning, the person will know everything.

Human society and individuals progress from a primitive or barbaric stage to a civilized stage. From the civilized stage, some extend themselves to become spiritualized. When spiritualization occurs, the real God is expressed. The religious "God" was born from human imagination; the real God is the child of individual spiritual attainment.

E. The Goal of the Post-Heaven Stage of Life Is to Be Good

The typical spiritual view of human nature divides human life into two stages; the pre-Heaven stage, before a person enters worldly experience, is pure goodness. The post-Heaven stage begins when a person starts to live his or her life. The goodness that manifests in the post-Heaven stage depends upon how a person reacts to internal and external pressure and the influence of one's family, school and social environment.

All people who live in the post-Heaven stage, especially when they are young, need to be guided. They can be guided to be good, but they also can be guided to be bad. Therefore, education, cultural habits and spiritual learning are important to assist people living in the turbulence of worldly life. Sometimes, people feel it is hard to stay upright in their lives. However, people are always rewarded spiritually by their upright life and deeds.

Due to the limitations of intelligence and vision, sometimes people still need to choose what is right for them. Yet, they should not overlook good spiritual support and guidance to maintain their life in a healthy and wholesome condition of mind, body and spirit.

People influence one another. Social leaders and their supporters always work to realize their goals. Even if their goals are good, the means they use to reach them are widely varied. It is important that each individual exercises his or her best influence while jointly working with others to accomplish a correct goal. Good works, good establishment and good or helpful human services, in a moral sense, are a great goal for all people to pursue and realize. Anything that is "good" in the abstract sense of the word is a moral and great goal in itself for all people to pursue and realize. What is good and how to reach good is a matter of self-education by keeping your mind and spirit continuously open.

5. Human Life Consists of Different Energies; the Mind Is Responsible for Shaping Them

Internally and externally, human life consists of the support of all organic conditions. Each individual is a small model of the universe and thus can learn about himself or herself from the universe. All people have the responsibility of learning how to attune their internal and external conditions to be able to function well in their daily lives. Internal conditions mean the individual self. External conditions mean one's companions, family and society. When people know how the elements of nature at large benefit or harm them, they can learn to adjust or attune themselves accordingly for the benefit of themselves and others. Nature provides a good example of attunement, because nature is constantly adjusting itself.

Nature itself is nothing. It is a melange, mixture, composition, combination or composite of different energies. When natural energy is harmoniously expressed, it is supportive to human life. When it is disharmoniously expressed, it is not supportive and can even be harmful to life.

Life itself is nothing. It, too, is the composition of different energies. When life is harmoniously expressed, it is beneficial. When it is disharmoniously expressed, it brings trouble to itself or others.

The Ultimate Spiritual Truth is nothing. The Natural Spiritual Truth is harmony. To learn Spiritual Truth is to learn harmony within and without life.

A. Human Mind and Social Fashion Reflect the Stage of the World which Deviates from Natural Health

When nature expresses itself with no extremely hot or cold days and gives wind and rain at the right times, vegetation grows well. Human population also grows and all good things enjoy prosperity. It is a great time for natural life. The ancient achieved ones used this model of nature to examine their own lives. This important symbolic standard was established for all aspects of life such as society, politics, economics, relationships, etc.

Nature can be a good model for understanding our lives. In individual emotions Spring expresses warmth and joy, Summer represents heat and over-excitement, Autumn represents wind and anger, and Winter represents cold and sorrow. The spiritual concept of living in everspring means to maintain an internal climate of personal warmth and joyful spiritual expression.

One can also find examples of moral nature or temperament from nature. Spring represents warmth, kindness and love. Summer represents fierceness, cruelty, tyranny, despotism, brutal strength, atrocious behavior, wildness and violence. Autumn represents stinginess, sternness, forbidding, discouragement and damage. Winter represents coldness and solemnity, gravity, severity and killing. Thus, Spring is the only standard for self-attunement.

In spiritual terminology, "Too much rain" means too much sex. "Drought" means lack of sex. "Flood" means emotional indulgence or too much enjoyment. "A volcano" represents fury. "An earthquake" means shock caused by an external situation. "Thunder" means scolding or punishment. "Cloudy" means moody. "A spring breeze" means joyfulness and goodwill, etc.

All people were born from nature. However, comparatively speaking, three types of people exist. The top level people are naturally balanced and are few in number. They do not need help or discipline. The second level of people rely on education and social guidance to become good. This level is the majority of people. The third level people need the help of the other two levels.

Balanced people are those who can give the most help. People who are soft are kind. People who are hard are abusive. In doing a task, only the people who are kind can set an upright purpose. They can also look for profit. They continually evaluate the merit of what they are accomplishing. They do not sacrifice truth for profit.

B. Governments Can Meet Nature

Nature is governed by the subtle law. The subtle law was discovered from nature; it is not separate from the deep nature. Most of the time, nature manifests as constancy and normalcy, but some of the time it appears to make trouble. That is only on the surface and has no depth. In human life, small natural troubles can be overcome. Disasters do not last long; every situation always returns to normalcy.

Human life is a small model of nature. Humans have troubles and make trouble. When the trouble is small, it is correctable. When the trouble is too big, it is destructive. It is better to take care of trouble when it is small rather than wait too long and be unable to correct it. Then, one only suffers from it.

On the scale of society, big disasters are created by ambitious leaders with incorrect intentions. In ancient times, these leaders came forward to depose former monarchs, causing much bloodshed and confusion in society.

The big mistake of recent times is the use of social force to strip individuals of their natural rights. Some social welfare programs have replaced the role which conventional religions did not fulfill. Such programs appear attractive to people with an idealistic nature, but they are not practical. They could serve some people on a small scale, like the ancient type of family or some religious group, etc., better than they could the people of an entire nation. When something like this is imposed upon a society, the organic condition of the society is naturally damaged.

Once a big disaster fell upon the people of some nations because certain leaders were enthusiastic about imposing a political social program upon the people. They were determined in their efforts, having the zeal of young religious leaders who have no practical experience in the world. In their absolute religious zeal, they expected a new paradise to be seen.

Practically, all social or political programs would do well to stay open to adjustment and revision. They can be tried out in an experimental stage on a small scale, using an objective spirit which allows for adaptation and change instead of an over-zealous religious spirit which tends to be blind to the obvious. Using unnaturalness to fight the naturalness of life always brings trouble and disaster. People cannot live in a society that is governed in an unnatural way. They cannot fully enjoy their lives if a society turns to be half-way natural.

People can live and enjoy themselves when life is natural. They do not mind paying the price of taxes to live in a country that does not give them undue hardships or burdens like other countries with ambitious leaders of incorrect intent. Thus, I conclude that democracy is a necessity to enjoying life. An extreme social program such as communism devitalizes society. It does not emphasize individual effort in a productive life, but emphasizes the equal obstruction of people's wealth, not out of healthy public spirit but from poisonous jealousy.

A good social program takes a small amount from ninety-nine people to give support to one person who is not able to take care of himself. This taking must be done only to meet circumstantial need. Such support need not be considered a meaningless obligation on the part of the givers.

6.   There Are Two Kinds of Energy: Helpful and Harmful

Each individual contains yin and yang energies. The words yin and yang are only symbols for two types of energy, they do not necessarily imply any application to womanly or manly energy. In the case of individual life, yang energy represents the spiritual energy of the individual and yin energy represents physical energy of the individual.

From the division of the one basic energy into the two energies of yin and yang, some accessory, supplementary, extra or noticeable attributes are brought about.   In the human sphere, physical or yin energy tends to be oriented toward sexual interest, or anything connected with physical interests. Spiritual or yang energy tends to be truthful or oriented toward anything connected with higher interests. Because both of these energies exist within each individual, the distinction between good and bad also exist in each individual.   This implies that yang, spiritual energy is good and yin, physical energy is bad.

If physical energy dominates a person, it does not mean that the person is big or strong. It means that the person has a certain type of influence in his or her life.   The dominant influence of physical energy within a person tends to manifest in one of two ways. One type is self-destructive and makes trouble for oneself, and the other is externally destructive and makes trouble for other people.

People who engage in individual spiritual cultivation with the goal of self-improvement and/or immortality need to watch the tendency of destructiveness and display self-discipline and self-control. The mind must be open to receive influence from above and to refuse the influence that comes from below. The mind is the one in the middle of the two energies.

A certain amount of need from the lower sphere is allowed to be fulfilled in a human life. However, a spiritual student never lets it become the dominating strength in his or her life being.

Some people are bad to themselves. The harm they cause themselves seems limited to themselves, but it might affect their whole family.

Some people are bad for others. When those people come together, it is a difficult time for the world. Big disaster will be brought about by them; all other people suffer. The world is natural, but culture is not 100% healthy. Evil people prey upon the culture too.

Human history is like a drunken giant walking on a path. Sometimes he staggers to the left and sometimes to the right. This gives the picture of the historical cycle of collective human nature as it moves from one extreme to the other. People suffer from lack of clarity in their spiritual vision. This happens when worldly or physical interest is too strong; then they can no longer guide themselves well in their lives.

An individual can be either helpful or harmful to the world or to one's immediate surroundings. However, one will never bring true happiness or lasting achievement to oneself or to the world without spiritual self-discipline.

In the external world, there are wars between different dark forces or the dark force fights the light force.

In the internal world, the same thing happens: there are wars between different dark forces or the dark force fights the light force. A peaceful internal world reduces the tendency toward physical expansion. In other words, when a person's desire for physical expansion - the desire to acquire material goods - causes too much pressure, the person usually becomes aggressive. When one learns to find peace internally, the life direction changes. The person will become more interested in helping other people improve their lives through their own efforts.

The person who cannot control his desire causes turmoil for the world and increases the darkness of society. The enlightened one of internal peace brings progress to civilization.

7. The T'ai Chi Diagram Represents the Universe
In the universe, the T'ai Chi Diagram expresses the ultimate law.

The diagram shows the harmony of two polarized forces. It presents the truth of interdependence of opposites and the co-existence of all lives. It even demonstrates the relationship between the two energies within an individual life or thing. The energy is one; the manifestations are two or many.

There are three spheres of universal reality: law, chi (energy) and form.

A. The Three Spheres of the Universe

The universe is integrated with three spheres. They are the subtle law, the primal energy and the forms.   They manifest like this in each individual existence:

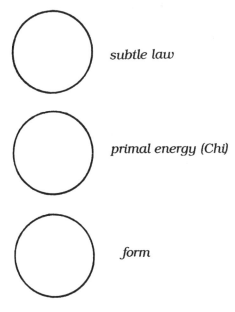

B. The Three Spheres Are Not Separate
This universal reality is also expressed like this:

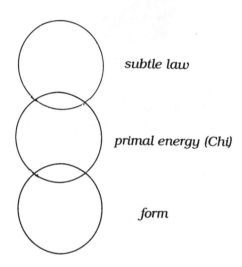

subtle law

primal energy (Chi)

form

This means the three spheres are integrated with one another. They are not separate existences. When normalcy and constancy are expressed, the integration of the three circles is presented.

Usually what is on the bottom represents what is deep, but these three figures or illustrations follow the symbolism of the *I Ching*. The *I Ching* develops upward, from the bottom toward boundless space; therefore the top is more subtle and deeper.

C. The Three Spheres Express Layers of Depth
Universal reality can also be expressed in the following way to express depth or gradation:

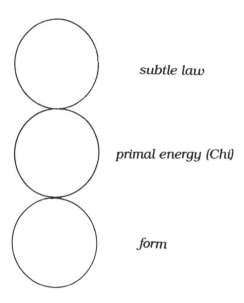

subtle law

primal energy (Chi)

form

D. All Three Spheres Must Exist in a Life
Truth is primal energy and desire comes from form. Some one-sided spiritual teachings suggest remaining with truth but destroying desire. This cannot be realized because life is made of desire. It is possible to reduce unnecessary desires which over-burden a life being. Balancing truth and desire is the main direction of living a good life.

8.   The Role of the Mind in Life and in the World
The internal knowledge of an individual human being can be unified with that person's external reality. This means that a person must be realistic about his or her ideas or that one's plans must fit the situation. Where internal knowledge exists without its external counterpart, a person tends toward subjective idealism. If a person over-relies upon the partial reality of

the external world without equally developing one's internal knowledge, there is a tendency toward blind materialism. Neither extreme brings any real benefit to life.

A person's worldly range is as big as one's mind can reach. The mind does not develop when it is limited by a small scope of external knowledge. Once a person's mind has developed fully, he or she understands that the world does not exist independently of the mind.

Universal law operates the universe. It is the same law that operates the mind of a person whose life meets the natural world. Universal law abides within primal energy. One's mind is part of universal primal energy when it realizes a normal life.

A harmful application of the mind occurs when the individual mind causes its own separation from the universal mind. This separation and the resulting selfishness damage the organic nature of the individual mind.

The entire world is one whole piece of energy. The pure, light energy is called spirits, and the impure, heavy energy is called the material sphere. Both are the universal life; together, they make up the universal life being.

9. The Subtle Law Is the Governor on the Level of Energy

The subtle law exists at all levels of energy, but only the most subtle energies are on the level of spirit. Even spiritual beings are governed by the subtle law.

People usually think that spiritual freedom is freedom of mind or freedom of thought. That is because people sense or intuit that the function of the mind is one expression of energy. However, the mind is still governed by the subtle law; therefore, freedom of thought and the freedom of using mind only happens when energy exists.

The ultimate law is T'ai Chi: the polarity of yang and yin and the harmony of both. This is also called the subtle law. No thought or use of the mind can go beyond the subtle law. Therefore, the one who is good at using the mind knows the law and uses the knowledge of the subtle law to guide one's thought. This will reach the harmony where no conflict exists. It is done on one level by seeing both sides of a situation.

The mind that does not see the law invites benefit or harm by the limitation of its development. The mind that effectively achieves a good result is the mind that reaches harmony. Harmony can be reached even in the use of mind; confrontation within the mind can be dissolved.

10. Life Is Movement; Natural Movement of Life is Renewal

The universe is energy. Energy is alive; it means life. Energy also means movement. There is nothing that is not moving. Things that do not move exist only on the relative level.

The universe does not die because it renews itself all the time. It keeps transforming to bring about the new. Individuals who know this reality and make universal nature their teacher also renew themselves and can last for a long time. Therefore, one of truth does not fear change, but brings about good change to oneself and to the world.

11. The Two Stages of the Universe

In the spiritual theory of the universe there are two stages.

A. Pre-Heaven Stage

In this stage, no objects are established.

B. Post-Heaven Stage

In this stage, things are relative. Objects are established.

C. The Integration of the Two Stages

All individual things have the three spheres of law, energy and form. In other words, they have both the Pre-Heaven and Post-Heaven stage existing simultaneously, and the subtle law which unites the two.

D. Each Individual Can Know Itself

From the division between the two stages and from the integration of the existence of the three spheres, each individual comes to know its life as distinct from other lives.

E. The Subtle Law Is the Highest Guidance

The subtle law suggests balance, harmony, cooperation, rationality and peace. This is the highest guidance of all lives, particularly human life, which is spiritually evolved.

12. The Mind Can Be Oriented Internally or Externally

In general understanding, there is a difference between the capability to know and the thing that is known. This assumption would tend to guide people's thoughts into the division of idealism and materialism.

In high spiritual reality, the capability of knowledge and the containment of knowledge are unified. By that, a person's external environment does not limit the expansion of the capability to know because a person can also know internally, intuitively. It is a defect of mind to attach or insist upon what has been known externally or intellectually and refuse what has not been known or seen. This creates religious beliefs.

The capability of knowledge and the range of knowledge continually develop. Their development comes together. I would like to give you a simple example. A boy who tended a group of ducks in my hometown to earn his living, only saw ducks. When he grew up, he joined the army. Years later, he became a general, and had more governing power to control more ducks. The horizon under his command was not the same, but the capability of knowledge of command developed.

This example of the boy and the ducks is an example of passive learning. For effective or active learning, one must develop the learning environment, such as schools, libraries, workshops, laboratories, etc. This leads to the development of the capability of knowledge. This type of learning environment helped the development of science.

In human cultural development, people in the Eastern hemisphere developed earlier than people in the Western hemisphere. Yet, the minds of Eastern people later became stagnant because they lacked natural inspiration like their ancestors who developed good spiritual knowledge and high art.

Minds of people in the Western hemisphere received natural inspiration while they also developed or created a learning environment; this led to modernization in science and techniques of mechanization. The shortcoming of intellectual knowledge as science was to overly externalize the mind. Modern scientists limit exploration to the external range of life and things. This still misses the integrity or wholeness of mind.

The natural tendency of people in the Eastern hemisphere is to internalize the external world. The natural tendency of people in the Western hemisphere is to externalize the internal world. Each is partial and thus must meet to be complete.

The learning of spiritual reality is to guide these two tendencies in the same person to meet each other. This is true not only on an individual level but also in the world culture.

The tendency of people to use only the right brain, which focuses externally, or left brain, which focuses internally, forms the two types of personality. They are the internalizing personality and the externalizing personality.

A person who is overly internal will miss the point of balance. This person usually cannot even support his or her own life. This person has no interest in improving society; thus, this person allows the forces of evil to manage society. This brings a passive life attitude. This has been exemplified by Eastern society, which is comprised of mostly internalizing personalities. Philosophically, this person will believe in occultism.

An overly external person will miss the point of balance, and will usually live up to an external standard or social fashion. This person will lack the essence of life, which leads to holding an aggressive life attitude. Philosophically, this person will believe in an external, almighty God.

These two trends express the nature of individual people as well as each society.

13. Righteousness or Doing Right Must Have Two Elements: Power and Correct Expression

Might must be right. If might is not right, it has an internal defect and will be short-lived. Irrational power is like a snowman on a summer day; it will not last long.

All powers in the relative sphere are converged forces. There is a time for each power to converge and there is a time for it to disperse. No matter what the nature of the power, whether it is a beneficial force or an evil force, all follow this law.

People who are dutiful in their lives look for no extra glory, only for correct fulfillment of their lives. People who strive for power are motivated by psychology or greed. To fulfill their social desires, they cause other people to suffer.

In all generations, evil forces form to create trouble for general people. The convergence of power, whether for evil or good, always attracts the participation of people. When power is evil, participants as well as objects of the power all suffer. As part of the force of evil, the participants feed poison to people, but at last they feed poison to themselves. There is repeated historical evidence that this it is a common mistake for people to be attracted to participate in the convergence of evil forces.

People of eternal truth discovered that in order for any power to last or survive, might must be the physical being of righteousness. In other words, righteousness or correct action can use physical force where necessary, and must do so, but with or without physical force, a thing must be correctly motivated. Might which is separate from righteousness is a mere temporal evil force. If righteousness is separate from might or power, because the righteousness is not complete, it cannot be realized or expressed. World and social progress must be brought about by the marriage of might and righteousness.

Might is not an instrument of religion. Sometimes a religion presents the unrealized righteousness, i.e., enemies of both sides ask help from the same god.

Righteousness is the spiritual development of all individual people; it must be expressed in order to be complete. If righteousness, or spiritual development, cannot be expressed in a society, the righteousness is not complete. One type of "saint" is imaginary; these are the people who leave the world to go to a monastery. They were never fully able to express their righteousness. Unless the world is a place where righteousness is fully expressed, no individual's concept saintliness is anything more than a religious emotional allurement. Real saints are the people in villages, towns and cities who bring about righteousness in life, whether to an individual or to society at large in the world position instead of adopting a religious position. A true saint has no personal motivation.

No act of righteousness should be valued; it is best to make righteousness itself become the greatest force or power in our everyday lives.

14. Can Human Nature Be Trusted?

In ancient Chinese philosophy, there was discussion about whether human nature is good or bad.

The philosophers who decided human nature is good directed the development of ethical establishments to make all relationships, whether natural or social, have an absolute one-sided obligation. This meant that people on the less powerful side must obey their superior, such as people to their king, a son to his parents, a wife to her husband, young brother to elder brother and younger friend to older friend. They must offer absolute obedience without questioning whether the decision of the upper side was correct, whether the behavior of their 'superior' earned their respect or the personality of the 'superior' was virtuous, etc. This idealistic ethic became a social discipline and was used by Chinese leaders to suppress the progress of Chinese society so that they could maintain control. This was what Confucius and Menfucius promoted.

The philosophers who decided that human nature is bad directed the development of evil means to control people. This directed the adoption of the Russian type of communist revolution in China as well as other events, such as the so-called ten-year cultural revolution, which was truthfully nothing more than a power struggle between two sides of leadership. The hypothesis that human nature is bad was fully expressed and demonstrated in some periods of history by leadership which lacked the vision to see the truth.

This hypothesis that human nature is bad was accepted by general society. People are too ready to accept any hypothesis as the ultimate truth; thus, this gives some leaders the opportunity to pursue manipulation of their immature and evil concepts. This of course lead to tremendous social disasters.

Whether human nature is good or bad cannot be determined or decided, because all human nature is developing. Human social nature or social behavior is like water used to irrigate crops; it can be guided east or west. Individual self-nature is the reality of one's spiritual development. It can be good, bad, or any combination of the two.

People can be evil because they are ignorant. People can be guided to be bad and to do bad if they have no personal spiritual development. The reality of life is that the hypothesis of whether human nature is good or bad has no use in general life. Neither point of view can be accepted as true, or accepted dogmatically, because human nature follows the subtle laws of energy.

We need to remember that since we were born into the world, not for one moment have we stopped forming ourselves spiritually and mentally. When this forming is coherent with natural development, it is right. When the forming is incoherent with natural development, it is self-destructive. Therefore, one's own spiritual nature grows and accomplishes itself each day without a cap or limit on its development in different directions.

15. Ji Is Produced by Subtly Harmonious Circumstances

Knowledge or intellectual or rational learning needs to be clearly separated from emotional forces such as belief, dislike or attachment to dogma. Knowledge can be allowed to grow with the capability of realizing the knowledge. The universe consists of a group of moving and transforming phenomena, just like the human world; thus, knowledge that is applicable to daily life should always be able to adjust to change.

In the teaching of the Integral Way, we do not exalt thoughts, ideas, plans or ready knowledge, etc. We think all those things are useful in assisting the accomplishment of a task or a goal but they are, of course, not the end or goal. We respect a special thing called "Ji." 機. Ji is a word which represents just the right moment, suitable environment, or supportive occasion which arises and makes it possible to do something. It means all conditions are correct for a seed to grow and bear fruit. Being able to see the Ji when it arises in circumstances or having the knowledge of Ji is a type of spiritual skill. Only a person who has a calm spirit can attain this ability. If you are impulsive, you cannot see the Ji, and your timing and actions will be off track. Thus, you will only bring about more mistakes and more suffering to yourself, and probably to your surroundings as well. The word "Ji" itself means wisdom.

Ji can be a chance, but it is more than chance, it can be an opportunity. It is even more than an opportunity. To see the Ji and to know the Ji, you need the cultivation of your pure spiritual energy, a quiet and calm mind. Even in a busy schedule and active lifestyle, the quiet and calm spirit is associated with the capability of seeing and catching the Ji. Otherwise, you depend on sheer luck. However, sheer luck is only successful part of the time. Sheer luck can make a scarecrow be a king, but it can also trap an intelligent person into trouble or strip a wealthy man of all his possessions.

There are many types of Ji, so even if you can see Ji, if you are not the right person, the Ji you can see might be useless to you. However, you may still be able to accomplish your goal under a good adviser.

For a person to have ambition which is compatible with his or her character or nature is the fuel of success. For a person to have ambitions incompatible with his nature, personality or character, and for that person to act upon those ambitions, will create a big disaster.

If the Ji of subtle circumstances are wrong, there is no absolute good way for a person to achieve his or her goal. If the Ji of subtle circumstances are correct, there is no bad outcome to a person trying to achieve a goal. Strong worldly leaders are able to see the Ji enabling them to climb high in their careers and obtain power, but they do not see the Ji in terms of implementing social policy to bring about benefit to people. Then they push impractical or incompatible ideas upon society. Thus, mistakes, trouble and sacrifice are created which last longer than their lifetimes. This can be exemplified by certain narrow religions, spiritual and social teachings and political or economic ideologies.

A perpetual struggle exists between accepting a new idea or belief and undoing the trouble of the previously accepted but harmful idea or belief. This is why attaining Spiritual Truth is so important. To learn Natural Spiritual Truth means to put away the dead knowledge, dogmas, ideas and belief by the attained capability of seeing the Ji. Success means the capability to see and realize the Ji. No true, good achievement happens any other way. Although people may explain how they arrived at success differently from using the term "Ji," they have used the spiritual function of seeing it, catching it, using it and realizing it. To learn spiritual reality is to nurture the "effectiveness" of your natural spirit to participate in the right action.

Chapter 6

Finding Gold in Sand:
Successful Spiritual Learning
Is Filtration

People may be born with good energy, but few people are born sages. This is why we need to improve our understanding of the world. Then, we can choose what is supportive to our lives. Master Chen Tuan was a person who did this, as did all highly achieved practitioners of the Integral Way. They all knew how to attain the essence of knowledge that would serve their own life and the lives of others. This attitude of learning is important, especially in the subject of spirituality.

The following text is meant to help you formulate the correct attitude toward learning spiritual truth. It also serves as an introduction and commentary on my own teaching. It may require concentration, but it is important.

I. The Nature of True Spiritual Teaching
The teaching of natural spiritual truth originated as the spiritual development of people when humans lived a natural life. The content of this development comprises the sciences of natural human life. In later times, the teaching was promoted as religions. My work serves to correct misunderstandings caused by overly externalized religions which cause people to lose the connection with their own spiritual nature. Thus, the teaching of natural spiritual truth is a guidepost toward the objective, correct direction when spiritual confusion arises from other religious teachings or the modern, unnatural way of life.

Unfortunately, as I have experienced, the true integral spirit of spiritual teaching has also disappeared from Chinese society. The government, society and individual lifestyle of China and later generations of Chinese people reflect the loss of spiritual balance. Yet the teaching of spiritual cultivation is dedicated to helping one to see and reach the spiritual nature in oneself.

The teaching of the Integral Way, which is sometimes called the teaching of Tao, expresses spiritual independence from any other spiritual teaching or religion. Unfortunately, some people use the word "Tao" for religious promotion among Chinese or other people. Those "folk" Taoisms are not the original teaching of spiritual truth as the sciences of natural human life; they are a mixed religion. Folk Taoism is not respected by educated Chinese people, who have opened themselves instead to Zahn (Zen) Buddhism which carries more spiritual essence than any other old custom. Zahn itself does not present the subtle spiritual origin as naturally as it is, because in Zahn spiritual teachings exist under the garment of religion.

Through teaching and publishing, I have worked to make the teaching of natural spiritual truth more understandable and serviceable to modern people through the Integral Way. Now, however, it seems important to point out that other teachers use the word "Tao," but their teaching is not necessarily related to the original development of teaching the subtle spiritual reality. I feel it is important to clarify the difference between other teachings and the teachings of the original spiritual truth. Some teachings are totally off-base, while others are just not deep enough. A few reach a good understanding. Although people are all at different stages in their evolution, there is a difference between teachings. Some of you will see the difference and others will not, but I feel I need to work on it.

I always encourage spiritual students to read and study widely so that, over time, they will understand what is true and valid and what is unimportant and false. Students who are careful enough will find conflict between what they are learning and the Integral Way as the science of natural human life I teach. They will touch upon the fact that the difference between the teaching of the Integral Way and religion is vast. Other teachers may have confused people who sincerely wish to learn something truthful to support their spiritual lives. Some do it intentionally and some do it innocently, because the teachers are victims of custom.

In part, my work is a response to the confusion caused by those teachers. The teaching of the Integral Way is the pure, broad spiritual development of all people, true spiritual growth that exists aside from conventional religious influence. It is not inconceivable that the world can experience a new epoch of harmonious spiritual life through deeper understanding of spiritual principles.

II. The Focus of a Spiritual Student

On a human level, it is natural that whatever a person does, someone will praise it and someone else will distrust it. How can a spiritual student deal with the praise and criticism that is received? Spiritually, you can only concentrate on what is right at your own stage. When you grow enough, both those who praise the teaching and those who attack it will understand it was truly their own problem, not yours.

It is difficult, but important, that a spiritual teaching maintain a flexible, open-minded approach to life. This is why any useful teaching values Lao Tzu's *Tao Teh Ching.* Lao Tzu is a model of high spiritual virtue. Unfortunately, some people who are called Taoist priests use his work with a rigid, religious intention. This is misleading to those seeking spiritual freedom.

If the material you use as a spiritual student is helpful to you, then stick with it. The teaching must stand on its own merit. As long as it is helpful to your life, then you must be moving in a right direction.

There are different kinds of teachings. Some are spiritual, some psychological, some emotional and some moral, and there are students who need to do some psychological work before directly pursuing spiritual learning and the useful knowledge of sciences of natural human life. Each student needs to find the teacher that is right for him or her.

Most of what I have presented as the teaching of Tao or the Integral Way was a secret or esoteric type of information in ancient times. At that time, the achievement of the spiritually developed ones was different from what was promoted on the social or cultural level. The social or cultural level teaches people ritual and ceremony, obedience and devotion. That may be important for some people, but it is not where learning ends. That is why my work teaches the essential achievement of the developed ancients. Some of my teaching is meant to help people have a clear spiritual vision, to see and understand things clearly in life. Some of my teaching points out how people can achieve themselves spiritually. This teaching explains the great and worthy achievements of our human ancestors.

My writings and teachings are a composite of many years of learning from my own personal spiritual cultivation and direct inspiration from the spiritual world. Both my own work and the inspiration of the ancients is dedicated to all human people who earnestly wish to improve their spiritual condition.

People with spiritual interest are supported in their search and in their lives by the spiritual realm through spiritual correspondence of the same energy. This support is given from the achieved human ancestors and the natural spirits in entirety. Certain knowledge or understanding is necessary for a person's individual achievement. Not all spiritual teachers or sincere social leaders share the same depth of the same knowledge. Not all of this special knowledge can be made public, because it was not written, although some related writings can be given. Having and mastering this knowledge is the test that proves true achievement.

Confusion about the source of spiritual teaching exists because some teachers are not genuine realizers of spiritual truth, but are socially skillful and can talk "Taoism" or religion without actually knowing or understanding it. They confuse others by talking about the source of the teachings rather than really helping people with their progress.

Not all teachers have achieved themselves or are even on the right path of life. This is why I say that each individual must use his own judgment in choosing to follow a certain teacher or adapt different teachings into his or her own learning system.

Here I would illustrate the approach of teachers. Once a Taoist teacher came to a new town to teach. The townspeople greeted him warmly. At the reception dinner, the teacher wished to demonstrate his personal value by saying: "My teacher can throw chopsticks into a stone wall a few inches deep and they can hardly be pulled out."

People marveled at this remark.

Some time later, another new teacher came to town. He was told about the story of the reception dinner. He responded: "My teacher can throw chopsticks to hit a wall many yards away and make them bounce off the wall and fly right back into his hand. Thus, he can continue eating food." All the people marvelled at this.

Years later, another teacher passed by the town. The hospitable townspeople offered him a reception dinner. They told him the two previous teachers' stories. He responded, "When I was a child, I used to throw my chopsticks at the wall while I was waiting for my mother to bring the food to the table. However, my parents stopped me from doing that. They said, 'Chopsticks are for eating rice.' I took that as the only truth. Otherwise, I would tell you that I can ride on my chopsticks and fly away." This third teacher was the earnest teacher. He was not interested in attracting attention by boasting or performing marvelous feats, but in the simple, true life.

When my sons heard this story, they told me, "Father, you do not even need to fly with chopsticks. There are chopsticks in most places of the world that you visit." They understand the value of a normal life, as do many, but not all, teachers.

III. A Good Policy of Spiritual Learning

Once I used the following story in another context. In the countryside of China, there was a temple. This temple was not tall but was magnificent in its ornamentation. The temple's hall had an offering table containing a pedestal with two idols sitting side by side. Above them was a wooden tablet describing who they were. On the left side of the tablet was written, "The God of Believing at Your Own Risk." On the right side of the tablet was written, "The God of Absolute Faith."

In front of the temple was a ditch. One day someone unable to cross the ditch moved the stronger looking idol off its pedestal in the temple and laid it across the ditch, enabling him to cross over. Seeing that this had happened, another man heaved a deep sigh and said, "How can the image of a god be treated with such disrespect?" He picked up the idol and cleaned it with his coat. Then he restored it to its original place on the right side of the offering table. He departed only after having bowed before it.

A spiritually developed man who was traveling by noticed what had happened with his spiritual vision. He then overheard another idol in the same temple address the God of Faith and say, "O great king, my friend, you are mighty enough to sit here and receive the offerings from many people as I do, but you have let yourself be humiliated by a foolish young man. Why not punish him for his affront by causing disasters to befall him?"

The God of Faith then replied, "Misfortune shall befall all those who henceforth offend me."

"What about the man who tramped over you and subjected you to utter humiliation?" responded the first. "Why not place a curse on him?   Why should misfortune befall only future worshippers and supplicants who appear before you in reverence instead of the one who has already offended you?"

The God of Faith replied: "The man who used my image to cross the ditch obviously did not have faith in being able to cross any better way. Since the man who desecrated my image did not have faith in me, how can I bring disaster to him?"

This illustrates how people with narrow religious faith would probably suffer trouble from having that narrow faith.

You need to know whether the teacher you learn from is a person of integrity and good character and will not misguide you or teach differently than what you are looking for. You put your energy into taking another person's advice and you do not wish to go down a wrong path. These are all matters of concern.

There are so many teachers. Some of them have received publicity for being overly aggressive politically, financially or sexually, or leading a large group of people to a foreign country and then inducing them into suicide. These are reasons for people to be cautious. You want to know that what you follow will take you to a good place or a different place.

Not all spiritual work is bad. Sometimes if work is good, nobody hears about it in the news report because quiet, good work does not usually make a sensational news story. Unfortunately, good work sometimes comes under the shadow cast by examples of disreputable teachers or negative reports by the press. That is the reason for this discussion; I wish to give you some advice: do not accept any spiritual teacher as a final authority for you. More important than accepting a teacher is to concentrate on the teaching itself and your own learning. In other words, your own independent learning is most important. It is all right to use a teacher, but do not let a teacher control your life or make that teacher be a god to you.

All teachers are in the position of teacher because what they promote receives a certain response from people. Each teacher's work has a slightly different focus, and while each meets a certain need, no one teaching can be judged as perfect. You can expect any teacher to be human and to be learning just like everybody else. If you have a rigid expectation about how a spiritual teacher is supposed to act, you will not be open to

learning the good things that the person has to teach you. It is
not necessary to learn everything from one teacher, because no
one teacher has mastered everything. Learn what is good and
helpful to you and leave the rest.

Trust your intuition about whether the teacher you are
learning from is giving something helpful to you. If you get a
feeling of "this is not right" then look for something else. It may
be that the material is not right for you, not that it is wrong. The
reason does not matter; just follow your deep inner promptings.

It is best not to concentrate too much on the teacher as a
person. Concentrate on what you can learn from the teacher's
work. Yet, one way to evaluate teachers is by how they apply
their beliefs to life. This is not always easy to judge because
personal expressions are different. Also, each teacher will have
some areas that they do not handle well and are still learning.

You see, people learn spiritually not only at different speeds,
but each person understands different aspects at different times.
Each person has different lessons to learn while on earth. A
student who criticizes somebody's teaching may not yet understand one part of the teacher's wisdom. A student who criticizes
a teacher in front of another person may be taking away
somebody else's chance to learn something important. Different
parts of any learning will benefit different people. Students need
to take what they can use from a teaching to help themselves
and then use their energy for their own positive work in the
world rather than passing judgment on the teacher. Allow other
people their learning opportunity.

If you decide that a certain teacher or tradition is not for
you, if it does not meet your standard or you cease to learn from
it, be respectful of the teacher and the teaching. Others have
something to learn there, so a quiet withdrawal is appropriate.

Spiritual books are offered for personal and group study.
Take what you can from any useful teaching, but avoid putting
any deep interest in the life of the teacher by becoming either a
fan or a critic. This is a good policy for learning from anyone's
material. Take what is good for you and ignore the rest.
Anything external that attracts your attention, such as the
details of somebody else's life, is a deviation from your forward
movement of learning.

IV. True Virtue Should Be Valued
More than Lineage or Tradition

A man weakened his eyesight by drinking too much. Once on his way home from town, he was crossing a bridge spanning a dry streambed and stumbled and fell off the edge. His hands held tightly to the railing; he believed that if he loosened his grip, he would fall into the depths and drown. A passerby who was in a hurry remarked, "You do not need to hold on so tightly; there is solid ground beneath the bridge."

The man did not believe him and, after clinging to the rail for a long time, he became exhausted. Finally, he let himself drop onto the bed of the stream and discovered that it was indeed solid ground. Getting up, he chuckled, "Why, had I known there was solid ground beneath, I could have spared myself this whole ordeal!"

People have strong faith in religions, and hold on as tightly as the man did to this bridge railing. They do not notice that there is safe dry ground under their own feet where they need to stand firmly.

Let us discuss how a spiritual teacher learns and becomes a person of certain spiritual achievement, able to teach and guide others. It takes a whole lifetime of study for a person to become a responsible teacher. At the beginning, a good teacher was a diligent student who was like a bee, gathering all the honey of knowledge and wisdom, even when facing a strong cold wind and rain in life. The student, before becoming a teacher, gathers the honey, then shares it with other people. That is the reality of a truthful spiritual teacher.

Some spiritual teachings are passed from teacher to student by the system of lineage. For example, in the monastery system, when the old abbot dies, the young abbot continues the teaching and meets the responsibilities of the position. They create a physical lineage.

In the tradition of spiritual truth, there are two ways that a lineage is created. One way is, as I mentioned, when people live in a monastery. Sometimes the physical type of lineage is a dead shell if the young abbot does not pick up the spiritual learning of the old one. Some do not. Then, no great service is produced for the world and people's spiritual vision is not improved.

Fortunately, some of these lineages do involve the passing of spiritual truth from an elder teacher to a student and are valid.

The second way to transfer learning is by spiritual lineage. In each generation, there may be some new spiritual teachers or sincere social leaders who rise up by their own spiritual aspiration. Such a person may base their teachings upon their successful spiritual achievement, and spiritual connection to or appreciation of past teachers. This means, as the *Tao Teh Ching* says, if you identify yourself with the subtle truth, you are the subtle truth. If you identify yourself with virtue, you are virtue. If you identify yourself with the lost one, you are the lost one. Therefore, if you identify yourself with someone's teaching, you are spiritually related to that teacher. However, spiritual learning goes a little deeper than that. It is not only a mental connection.

Master Zhang Dao Ling, 34-156 A.D., initiated the Heavenly Teacher School or exorcist's Taoism. It has been actively practiced by Chinese folks since the late Han Dynasty. Zhang Dao Ling declared that Lao Tzu descended, taught him and authorized him to continue teaching the practices of spiritual truth. Lao Tzu was active during the Chou Dynasty (1122-256 B.C.), at least 600 years before Zhang Dao Ling was born (34 A.D.). It is not for me to decide whether he directly saw or met Lao Tzu. Zhang Dao Ling asked five bushels of rice from any student who wished to learn his practice. By doing that, he gathered people and collected as much grain as a mountain. In the end, the accumulation of grain enabled the gathering of people to become an armed rebellion. Therefore, later Master Kou Shuan of the period of Three Kingdoms (220-264 A.D.) and his grand nephew Master Kou Hong of the Jing Dynasty (265-419 A.D.) refused to recognize his practice as having been part of the true spiritual heritage. They have their own spiritual school, also as the practice of self-cultivation.

During the later Jing Dynasty, the Northern Wei Dynasty (223-535 A.D.) was established in northern China. The Wei dynasty formally adopted Taoism as a religion. A new Heavenly teacher, Master Qu Chyen Tsi, arose at this time. He also declared that Lao Tzu had descended from Heaven to teach him and gave him a collection of books containing corrections of some of Master Zhang Dao Ling's teaching mistakes. Again I cannot comment upon whether Qu Chyen Tsi received Lao Tzu's teaching. This would have occurred 1,000 years after Lao Tzu's active time.

Each of those two masters was involved in religious movements. Their approach to serving people was different from mine. I cherish truthful teaching and achievements of the ancient developed ones of all times. The unity of spirit of their wisdom has become the spiritual support for my teaching work.

In the earliest time, there was Pu Ku's Taoism. Then there came the Taoism of Three Gods: Heaven, Earth and People (they were human leaders). Then there came Fu Shi's Taoism, then Shen Nung's Taoism, then the Yellow Emperor's Taoism. I accept the essential achievement of all ancient people as a broad spiritual teaching, as Lao Tzu and Chuang Tzu did, to continue the spirit but not the specific social establishment of one time or any time. I would not do what religious leaders do by presenting the spiritual growth of only one stage of human development. What I present is the spiritual development of all stages; the entirety of integral spiritual development. I do not take advantage of people's spiritual under-development to establish any worldly power. I recognize all ancient achieved ones as the background of people's possible achievement rather than limitedly focusing upon one or several individuals. All ancient achieved ones are the background of my achievement, and therefore I serve people the same way I developed and learned.

I would also like to give you a historical example. The later four main schools of immortal Taoism, South, North, West and East, each arose at a different time. The north branch of Immortal Taoism is the representative of this religion so far by its prosperity and popularity. The initiating teacher of each school mentioned that he had met Master Lu, Tung Ping (798 - ? A.D.) personally. Zhang Tsi-Yang, the initiating teacher of the Southern School, lived from 984 to 1082 A.D. Lee Hang-Shu, the initiating teacher of the Eastern School, and Lu Chyan Shu, the initiating teacher of the Western School, left no record of their dates, but lived some time during the Sung Dynasty, 960 to 1279 A.D. Wahn Chun-Yang, the initiating teacher of the Northern school, lived from 1120 to 1170 A.D. According to scholastic attitudes and truthful examination, the time period when Master Lu, Tung Ping was alive and when the schools were initiated were far apart. However, what is impossible to ordinary people is possible to religious Taoists. It was the religious skill of the teachers who made the spiritual connection with Master Lu, Tung Ping and have made people accept that.

Thus, one of the ways of passing teaching is through spiritual lineage. A student can continue the teachings of a past teacher by spiritual identification or spiritual inspiration. This can happen even if the teacher lived many generations ago. It is not strange; it is common in this tradition.

There is a third way of transferring teachings. Some individuals who are not connected to any tradition or religion learn spontaneously from nature. Perhaps they read books of different spiritual orientations. They have no physical teacher nor connection with any established spiritual teaching. Some of them become teachers, but others do not.

Many students want to know if the attainment of deep spirituality happens naturally or whether it is passed from teacher to student by special transmission in a lineage. Both are true. It can happen naturally by personal self-education and natural inspiration.

In modern times, most people need a teacher's help, directly or indirectly, so that they are not confused as they move forward in their growth. The modern world is confusing. Mostly a teacher helps a student change old bad habits by pointing them out, but it is still up to the student to follow the teacher's advice.

Spiritual achievement usually requires a great deal of study. It also requires that a person change or eliminate certain life habits, but spiritual achievement is more than studying, acquiring knowledge, and changing habits. Some people study a lot and are not achieved. Others improve their habits and are not achieved. I would say that both are requirements, but neither is the spiritual achievement. It is still deeper than that.

How can a student tell without looking at credentials whether a teacher has bona fide spiritual achievement? By reading and testing the teaching material offered. If it works for you and you feel benefitted, with increased clarity and more understanding, that is good. If you feel that you are making some progress in your life, even if things are more challenging, that is a good sign.

If a teaching does not seem to be right for you, keep in mind that each person has a different way of learning. For example, a person with an history of incarnations in the tradition of Christianity might not do well with truthful Taoist or deep spiritual teachings. This does not mean the teaching is not good, it just means that it does not meet that person's spiritual heritage. This is why I suggest that a student read material from several different traditions to find one that seems to fit before becoming involved or investing time and energy.

In the tradition of the Integral Way, the expression of each individual teacher's natural inspiration becomes a different message according to the times. It establishes the teacher's name, authority and image. Thus, each new teacher of each new generation has a new expression according to the social background. They support the tradition but express it differently through their own personal achievement and message. They support what they feel is proper to support and eliminate some expression that is unrelated to their times. Thus, a new teacher offers a refreshed teaching of the traditional spirit. Practically, it is a teacher's spiritual virtue to revive the traditional spirits with a new expression. This is the reality of becoming a great teacher.

Different teachers utilize the traditional authority to help them make a living. Some teachers have not caught the spirit of the tradition but work on the level of the material objects or intellectual understandings. Not all teachers are on the level of the inspired great ones of the age. Lesser teachers, if they are virtuous and do not allow personal insecurity or jealousy of the great ones to destroy their good characters, can still make an important contribution. Unfortunately, there are also those who try to use negative means to attract students, such as through telling rumors about other teachers or creating scandals. Please beware of the teachers who do so and also do not take any stories as ultimate truth.

A rumor or scandal is given by one person. Regardless of whether the words are true, if they stick in your mind, your view of the teacher or political leader is colored by that rumor. It is better not to believe something that someone else said and hold that as your opinion of another person. For example, once someone came from town and told the mother of Chen Tzu that her son killed someone in town. The mother had confidence in her son's high moral character, so she denied it. Soon after that, a second person came to the mother and said, your son killed someone in town. That began to make the mother have a small doubt. The third time someone told her, your son killed someone in town, the mother's confidence in the good character of the son was shaken. She became worried and disturbed. She did not know what to do. She began to feel that her son had caused her some disgrace. She was agitated about this matter until the fourth person came to tell her, someone killed somebody else in town today. The killer is a good friend of your son and his name is also Chen Tzu. The mother relaxed and sighed, saying, if three people came to say that your son killed somebody, even his own mother would not trust the character of her son any more. Chen Tzu was a famous moral person in his time.

There is a proverb in Chinese that says, three persons can make a tiger out of their mouth. During the time this saying originated, China was quite rural and there were tigers. It means that if three people say there is a tiger, other people will all react as though the tiger were real. People will trust this nonsense because they do not know any better or they do not have all the facts.

I give these two examples to help you understand about trusting other people's words.

Natural inspiration was received by sages thousands of years ago and by other people thousands of years later in a different place and different time. The natural inspiration and the spiritual quality is the same, but the expression is different. Those who truly continue the spirit of the Integral Way value their own spiritual inspiration and correctly express it in the new teaching rather than using negative means to attract students.

I hope this gives you some insight about a teacher's credentials or authority. You do not need to feel uncertain about a lineage. You can receive the natural inspiration directly by yourself. This is how the learning of spiritual reality differs from worldly religions.

V. People Carry Spiritual Truth

There was a Taoist priest who sold blessing charms to support his life and his drinking habit. The charms he sold were supposed to have magic power. Once he solicited a purchase from a young scholar who knew him. The scholar declined and answered him straightly, saying, "Pardon me, but I think you need it yourself more than I do." The Taoist priest said, "I always make a sale to those who ask more than I do from life."

The scholar obviously did better than the priest, but did not buy the charm.

There are two kinds of tradition. One is a true tradition. The true Integral Way is a culture or broad spiritual education. The true Integral Way is fulfillment of universal life. Spiritual Truth is absolute truth or the development in reaching the truth. Spiritual Reality is the integral Truth. The Integral Way is unified truth. The subtle origin is immortal and eternal. Its existence does not depend upon shape or name, because shape and name categorize things. Categories are changeable or "interruptible"; therefore, they are not eternal. Shape and name exist on the worldly level, the physical sphere, which is the variable sphere of the world. That sphere is always subject to change.

Absolute spirit is nothing. Nothing does not mean nothing at all. It means the universal subtle energy. It has not been formed as lives or shapes and things. Everything in the world comes from 'nothing.' In other words, all something comes out of nothing. Life itself changes from nothingness to become something. This is a little hard to explain to you, because when you were born, the world was already there. Where were you before you were born? You cannot remember with your mind, but you still have your spiritual trust. You were a nature spirit, but where were you before you were a nature spirit? All levels of beingness come from non-beingness.

All religions, likewise, are something made out of nothing. A true student values not only the things important to life, but also the nothingness. The students who are less developed stay attached to things that exist.

Therefore, nothingness is called true tradition. I can never deny the true tradition, but I can deny the external establishments that try to describe it. Taoism and other religions both serve the function of spiritual education in human life.

When you learn or teach spirituality, the most important thing is to break away from the external establishment. Once there is too much establishment and too much cosmetics or decoration, people become confused. They hardly know which way is right and which way is wrong. This is the difference between religions and sciences. Religions are cosmetic, while sciences as I illustrated are objective.

If you know that everything comes out of nothing as the subtlety of universal reality, then you understand that nothingness or the unformed and unshaped subtlety is the root. Thus, you do not need to start searching or pursuing spiritual truth by going anywhere, because where you are is spiritual truth. Nothing exists everywhere. That is the absolute truth.

You may ask, "If spiritual reality is nothing, how does it give service?" As I have implied, the subtle truth is not nothing, but that is the way to describe it. There are two ways to know the subtle origin. One is through its substance, and the other is through its function or creation. The function or creation is the usage of something. Let us say you have $100 in your pocket and decide to go shopping. You go to the store and buy what you need. Each person who goes shopping has different needs, so each uses money in a different way. The original $100 dollars and what you buy with it are two ends of the same pole. The $100 is the substance, and the items purchased are the function or the creation.

To cultivate oneself is to nurture the potence of universal life. Then naturally, according to your need and wisdom, you can apply what you nurture or cultivate. That is still in the second level, not the highest level, because any thing or money is something consumable, as well as a life. Spirit is not consumable; it is inexhaustible. Life is exhaustible; spirit is not. That is the difference you need to know. If spiritual reality is nothing, how does it give service? It gives service through people who have attained it, or people who do not even know the word Tao but have the same universal unbiased virtue.

The most important thing to one who wants to teach is to continue the true tradition or the true discovery. It is not necessary to continue the external lineage, because that is changeable or interruptible. The true tradition can never be interrupted.

Many years ago, a teacher came to the world and taught the high truth. Then, physically, he disappeared, complying with the natural law of death. His death only happened on the low sphere, because his spirit still exists. This is why it can happen that many generations later, another teacher is born who teaches the same thing. Do the two people have a connection? Physically no, but their spirit is one. All achieved masters are one person, one beingness. If you embrace, respect and cultivate spiritual reality, you are maintaining or carrying the tradition.

Still, if you emphasize this master or that master, you are just talking names. You can also give yourself, if you like, a thousand names. In English, there exists the word laughter. In Chinese, the word for laughter is shiaw. In French it is rire. In Spanish it is risa. In German, it is gelachter. No matter what it is called, laughter is the same physical reaction from a similar type of stimulation. In a different place it is described differently by using a different word; that's the only difference. Maybe different generations change the wording or description for laughter too. It is not hard for me to give up the word "Tao," if I could find a better word to help your understanding in doing my job.

It is not important to follow an established teacher or name in order to practice your spiritual cultivation. The most important thing is to have real devotion to the true teaching that embraces the entire spiritual truth. Spiritually, being known and recognized as a physical being or a name is not important. The real spirit is important; it exists forever.

VI. Learning the Essence

In the past, I have been introduced on the covers of my books as "heir to the wisdom and experience transmitted through an unbroken succession of seventy-four generations of Taoist masters dating back to the Han Dynasty." This is a limited description. It is my spiritual reality to choose to continue the original spirit of ancient achieved ones throughout millions of years, and the free and independent spirit of all my forerunners in this past 2,500 years.

In today's religious market, many people declare they are Taoist teachers or students. The social rank of Chinese conventional society was arranged in a hierarchy with scholars on top, then farmers, skilled people and business people on the bottom. The old society respected scholars most highly because only scholars had an opportunity to become royal officials and partake of the ruling system. Spiritual learning had no social position at all because it served people in a different way than in their worldly practical life; at least that is how people viewed it. It was foolish then, and it is still foolish now, to describe one's spiritual learning in front of people because it does not give a person any social status. Only if you are an established teacher do you wish to describe your learning, and even then only in a limited way.

In spiritual teaching, more important than anything else is giving authentic teaching based on actual spiritual achievement. Anyone who wants to can trace the lineage of my tradition. The names of teachers of Sun Ching School, different sects of the Golden Immortal School (my father was related to those schools and with our family tradition) and the Jing Ming School (my mother was related to that school) in different generations were recorded in the *Taoist Canon*, the collection of 1487 spiritual books. Although the *Taoist Canon* has enormous volumes, it still cannot include all the teachings and all the names of the people in spiritual activity during the last 5,000 years. There are still other collections of scattered Taoist spiritual books, which can serve as a partial reference. This collection was compiled between 1436 and 1446 A.D. during the Ming Dynasty.

We can also see from the larger portion of that big collection that many teachers in the last 2,500 years rigidified the vivacious spirit of the subtle origin, Tao. Tao is what describes the liveliness and spiritedness of universal natural life. An overly religious approach brings about the destruction of the organic condition of healthy life. It is against spiritual principles.

Practically, in the past 1,500 years, the initiating Zahn (Zen) masters and some later Zahn masters preserved the teaching of Lao Tzu and Chuang Tzu much more than did religious Taoism and folk Taoism. In Chinese society, people give more respect to Zahn Buddhism than they give to religious and folk Taoism, because those expressions of Taoism did not help people's spiritual growth; their leaders took advantage of people's ignorance.

My parents' spiritual learning during their youth was aided by their elders. Those elders had learned from one or more spiritual schools or religious sects; therefore, most of the spiritual teachings were related to one another. Those teachers did not build up any particular prejudice for any particular school or religious sect because they are all connected or inter-related. It is also not necessary for a student to limit oneself to a particular school until the student has grown sufficiently to make a commitment to a truthful, useful and helpful spiritual teaching.

During thousands of years many religions, many schools, sects and independent teachers were developed. They are just like the small streams that flow toward the ocean of Tao or the Subtle Origin. The Subtle Origin is the real spiritual source for all true spiritual teachers and students. Thus I advise you to avoid rigidly accepting only one teacher or another, because this brings about differences that split people religiously. Recognize only the broad universal spirituality. Study the teachings of many teachers as the different descriptions.

The work of my direction is simply to present you with the Integral Truth and the essence of all teachings. All good and open teachers guide their students toward the common spiritual source. The main difference among teachers is their maturity and the presentation of their personal attainment. By this, I mean there are teachers in different stages who meet the need of different situations and different levels of students.

The work I choose to do is to assist your own spiritual growth and maintain the naturalness of your life. A bad tradition is like the Chinese custom which promoted women to bind their feet, thus damaging naturalness for the sake of fashion. Spiritual students can go through religious discipline, but sometimes, if they stick with it too long, it is like a woman binding her feet. Even if she stops, her feet have already been affected.

The dividing line between the Integral Way as the teaching of Lao Tzu and Chuang Tzu, etc., and religious or folk Taoism as the later developed religions which also used those teachings, is the motive or intention. The true tradition gives the teaching. The false may wish to control people and may take advantage of their psychological weakness and ignorance or mixed approach.

It may not aim to help; it aims to cheat and rule or has a mixed purpose. There is also a dividing line between being religious and being spiritual. Being religious means to be attached to dogmatic teachings. Being spiritual means to be open to true knowledge and one's own spiritual inspiration in a realistic process of improving oneself.

For many years, the following metaphor was used: You use a ferry boat to cross the water. Once you cross the water and reach dry land, you do not need to carry the ferry boat on your back. Let us apply that maxim to spiritual teaching: You use the teacher, but you do not have to take the teacher as a burden. The maximum function of a teacher is to support you and assist your spiritual growth without personal establishment, personal demands or asking anything from you.

Thus, I hope people take the best of any good teaching and use it to improve their lives. The true value of a teaching is in the service that it gives to people, not in worn-out credentials. It is my sincere wish that students stop looking at the superficial and go into the depth.

If you have the ambition to learn and continue the true spiritual teaching, all truly achieved teachers in all lineages will be reached and connected.

VI. Commitment Only to Self-Improvement

The tyrant Emperor Wu Di of the Han Dynasty received as tribute a wine known as the elixir of immortality. His guard, General Dongfang Shuo (who was a spiritually developed person, although this was not recognized by others), took the wine and drank it himself. This enraged the emperor, who intended to execute him for it. Dongfang Shuo told him, "What I have drunk is supposed to make me immortal. Therefore, I cannot be executed. If I die, that would certainly show that such wine cannot live up to its name." With this, he wished to suggest to the emperor that immortal medicine is internal, not external.

Spiritual teaching is not easy because so many things can be misunderstood. Teaching can be done in many ways. I have talked in my other books at length about this topic, but I would like to clarify some points so that you can understand better.

The Integral Way should be a broad spiritual service to all people. As a specific practice in the past, this tradition has been known for the system of a teacher adopting students. It still does. In general, the Integral Way is undiscriminating service; this has always been the way. My teaching activity in the world adopted students under the system of no commitment. I have always adopted this system because I feel that students need some freedom in learning. Also, no teacher can be responsible for the achievement of a student. Some learn and others do not. I give freedom to find what works best for them. If I can be of some service to other people in their stage of growth, I feel that I have done my job. If people are not growing with my teaching, for example, if they are not ready or are at a different stage, I would prefer they find what can help them rather than stay and be unhappy.

The teacher-student system does not totally work in modern times the same way it did in ancient times. In ancient times, a student had to walk for days and then go searching in the high mountains even to find a teacher. Today, they take an airplane, which is much easier, but not all students find the appropriate teacher. Fortunately, it is not necessary for each student to go to a teacher. For some it is. Each student has to find the level of teaching that fits his or her need. Also, each individual has the need for individual growth.

Most of the time I am encouraged by serious students who are looking for something to help their own spiritual growth. I am encouraged, so I continue to offer my work.

Traditionally, teaching spiritual truth is not done for financial purposes; it is a service. How a teacher took support from students was different; usually there was a donation. In worldly life of modern times, spiritual teachers can ask financial support. I believe it is correct for those teachers to charge fairly for any teaching materials. Any good teaching can adopt the best policy for sustaining their good work.

My personal teaching is a spiritual service rather than a career to earn my living. I do not say all teachers must work in my way. Fair support for good teaching is important. During this troubled time of human society, all of us can offer to do our share to help human spiritual progress. All can work without motives of competition, scheming, manipulation or pursuit of

power. When a name is given, it expresses personal responsibility for the work. If your work creates the feeling of insecurity in
some other jealous or short-visioned teachers, your power has
not reached them because they encage themselves too tightly.

A good teaching work does not aim at earning a living. Yet,
any type of good work can bring a good side product to the world
which can be viewed as a service. As a teacher, you are looking
to help the world become more peaceful and orderly, and to help
all people attain clear spiritual vision. The world has suffered
enough from dictatorship, gangster-type political behavior like
communism, and tyranny. This is why you cannot teach in any
way that is different from an open, flexible approach. Rather
than wish to be a "spiritual teacher-lord" over other people, you
offer what you have achieved from your practical life and
spiritual learning. A good teacher gives each person the space
and freedom to learn in an individual way and at an individual
speed.

VII. Breaking off the Boundary

Once there was a man extremely fond of hearing praise from
the mouths of others. A Taoist priest who was famous for being
a physiognomist (someone who can tell another person's fortune
by observing his physical features), noticing this aspect of his
character, spoke highly of him in his presence to win the man's
attention. He said: "Your bright eyes are indicative of a won-
drous fortune throughout your life." The man was taken with
this remark and feasted the physiognomist for days, even
lavishing expensive gifts upon him. When they were about to
part, however, the Taoist priest had a disturbed conscience and
told him, "There is one thing you ought to keep in mind." "What
is it?" asked the man. "You really need to find a vocation! A
pair of eyes is hardly enough to see through anyone! Your bright
eyes can hardly see reality," replied the physiognomist.

A spiritually responsible teacher is a person who is in a
position to offer something to help other people. What we can
learn from the ancient masters such as Kou Hong, Lu Tung Ping
or Chen Tuan is to understand their life experience and achievement. We can learn their philosophy and spiritual contribution.
Their achievement can receive our personal admiration and
appreciation, and thus our spiritual identification.

Although it is helpful to have an achieved teacher, and some lineages are valid, lineage is not the most important thing. When a man comes to a new town as a stranger, if he describes the kind of family he comes from, the famous relatives he has and the wealth of his inheritance, he is only talking about the past; the new town does not take these expired credit cards. Similarly, a spiritual lineage is also of the past. The present is what is important; you are looking for teachers who have achieved themselves.

Showing off one's lineage to boast of one's spirituality is like holding up a big dinosaur bone to show people the glory of the dead past. Many teachers have lost the vision to nurture the true, alive dinosaur, meaning spiritual energy. My experience with spiritual teachings is that even with a tradition or lineage, all teachings need to be renewed or rejuvenated.

I do not promote an attachment to lineage. The heritage belongs to the people who appreciate it. This is the true nature of the teaching of the Integral Way or Integral Truth. Integral means complete. Thus, integral truth includes all schools and all achieved masters of the past, present and future, not just one school. A teacher who conforms or is confined to only one school or one lineage passes down narrow knowledge. Such a limitation is not beneficial. It does not offer enough variety to express spiritual abundance and serve all people. It is better to keep a broad attitude than a narrow one.

In my teaching, often the teaching of ancient developed people is quoted. The "ancient developed people" as a title is similar to the title of God or Buddha in other traditions, and they are also included. Some ancient developed ones carry no name. By this I mean that they did not become famous enough for their name to become known to either ancient or modern people. They were farmers, boatmen, blacksmiths, housewives, mothers, etc. They had not earned a name, but still deserve the respect and admiration of true students.

The teaching of Integral Truth originated by ancient achieved ones. It is followed by those who give up rigid adherence to traditions or the creation of new schools of divergent thoughts.

A student can enjoy the many different backgrounds of all highly achieved spiritual masters, named and unnamed, but for all of them, it is important to hold one standard. The master must have been self-achieved through natural inspiration, and the method used is how the achievement was accomplished. It is not necessarily helpful to emulate or appreciate leaders who are motivated to start a religion or give spiritual teaching in order to organize followers, to group people or to rule a society. No religion or teaching can include all teachers and all sages. Not only that, it is suitable to learn only from those who were natural in spirit. It is not necessary to focus upon those who organized programs and teachings unless, of course, that is also your interest. If you do so, be sure to examine the teachers' motivations. Natural inspiration can still be organized and is provable to certain people.

The beauty of studying many different teachings is to see the different forms and learn from comparing the similarities and differences. Undeniably the oriental religions are different from the Western religions, but Tao or the Integral Truth has no east or west. When an oriental religion is brought to the West, it is totally new. It can be taught without the traditional rituals because the time and culture are different.

There have been many teachers of Taoism and other religions. Their material still exists, but not all of it is valuable. It is important for any student to filter out what is old or already dead or unnecessary from the culture of Taoism or others. It is most important to learn the essence of all achievement from the broad scale of the old culture of China and all the other countries which had a spiritual teaching and also learn the modern-day teachings.

VIII. Be Choosy in Your Acceptance

Once three people were sitting close together in the winter sunlight trying to warm up. After some time, they became warmer. The one sitting in the middle suddenly had an itch on his back. He asked his companion on the right to scratch it for him. His friend tried twice, but failed to locate it. The man then asked the companion on his left to do the same, but she too, failed to locate it even after five separate tries. Disgruntled, the man complained, "All friends are supposed to have intimate knowledge of their close friend. How, then, can they fail me in this simple request?" He then tried scratching it with his own hand and found the spot easily. Why could he do it so readily?

Because with an itch, as with other things, a person always knows himself better than other people know him.

Another important principle is that written teachings be offered in a selfless way, without feelings of personal power or manipulation.

An achieved teacher does not wish to establish his or her own name. The teacher may give service to others, but without giving a name. One's name may be offered as a means for people to identify the teaching, a kind of reference. A good teacher does not look for personal establishment. The teacher accepts responsibility for one's actions rather than merely trying to establish oneself as a social leader as a goal. A good teacher does not ask for personal worship from any student.

You can forget that someone was your teacher, but still see what real benefit is brought into your life through what you have learned from the school. When you become the master of great life, you are the one I respect. Your becoming the master of your own great life is more important than superficially ranking yourself in a lineage.

The topic of sex is something that comes up for all spiritual teachings. This is because sexual energy is the foundation of spiritual growth. Some teachers abuse it. It is best that a teaching does not have a stiff attitude toward sex, but discipline is important. Anyone engaging in spiritual learning must not have a loose attitude toward sex. If one has a suitable sexual expression, it is important to know the right way to do it, and what is beneficial and correct for oneself and one's partner. This is the correct sexual attitude at the stage of an achieved spiritual person.

When you sell something, buy property, conduct business, have a relationship with a spouse or mate or teach spiritual learning, a fair trade needs to be made. You must follow the correct legal and socially acceptable process in handling that matter. It matters less what people say about you and more to know that your way of doing things is straightforward and earnest. Being earnest is the best policy. Earnestness and following the social norm are practical measures and attitudes that need to be adopted not only by spiritual adepts, but also by general society. If people say something untrue about you, it is because they do not know you. Or it is because they do not have any experience in doing this type of work and cannot understand how it must be done to be correct. All teachers and students can always follow the guideline of earnestness.

All people live in the relative plane of life. We can only work on ourselves to avoid any moral defect and spiritual imbalance. Working on ourselves is similar to driving a car. Although you may be a dutiful driver, you still cannot say your driving is accident proof. Although you do not take drugs or drink alcohol when you drive, somebody else might, so be careful. When your emotions are different, your driving is different too. In all aspects of life, you need to watch yourself and require yourself not to be overly confident when you move on the life path.

People have trouble. People have stories to tell. A spiritual teacher is somewhat a public figure. I do not think a spiritual teacher should use his energy just to protect his name or argue for his own righteousness at all times regarding all matters. In the world, some people enjoy a better reputation than their character deserves and some people suffer from bad reputation but it does not mean the true character of that person has failed.

Sometimes you would feel that it is a nuisance being disturbed or having one's personal reputation damaged by gossip. In spiritual cultivation, one direction we wish to work on in improving ourselves is to be a true person. If a person is truly achieved, right and wrong can be determined deeply by this person's own recognition. Abide with what is right and correct what is wrong without extending yourself to yell in the streets, saying "I'm right, I'm perfect, I'm the only one of righteousness." That would push oneself in the direction of being an impostor and hypocrite. That is what general society and ordinary culture promote.

A true spiritual person works on oneself and values holding the firmness of a real character. A true spiritual teacher is never bothered too much by the gossip of the world. Spiritual teachers or sincere social leaders offer what they can give. Your efforts to help the world bring the respect and trust of some as well as jealousy, irresponsible speech and groundless rumors of others. This is the world. No one has the time or energy to fight all of this. If you always fight it, you cannot concentrate on achieving your goal or doing good work for the people who need your kind of help.

If you are the recipient of rumors about someone, know that they may not be true. Gossip is rarely true. Gossip usually represents the level of the people who spread it, so I do not suggest that you evaluate a teaching by gossip.

Look up at the sky. The bright sun and moon are there. Sometimes they are covered by clouds. However, the clouds never stay all the time; they go away. The clouds never really cover the sun and moon. Some people cannot enjoy the brightness of the sun and moon because of the location they are in. The truth, like the sun and moon, is always bright and uncovered by any clouds, but worldly people cannot see them all the time.   It is not the problem of the sun and moon; it is the position of some people.

If you are a spiritual teacher, you are also a spiritual student. In his bosom, a spiritual student always enjoys the cloudless sky. Look at the beautiful, far-reaching, unobstructable cloudless sky. It is the symbol of a clear mind. This presents a spiritual reality which all spiritual students can pursue.

IX. Spiritual Reality Is a Thoroughfare to All

Spiritually, West and East must meet. The West tends more toward external establishment. The East tends more toward internal inspiration. In deep truth, there is no external that has no internal. Also, there is no internal that has no external. It is the tendency of the human mind that over-building externally does not inspire people to reach the deep internal truth. Also, working too deeply spiritually neglects the importance of the external world. Both the internal and external seem interdependent; this is the new direction for universal spiritual attainment.

The following points outline my teaching that I have reached:

1. Recognize the universal spiritual nature. It is called such by the achieved ones.

2.   The developed concept of God, through generations, has practically become another name for the spiritual nature of all people in a broad sense as the function or as one expression of the universal spiritual virtue.

3. The universal spiritual nature is eternal or immortal. It is the generating force of the universe. That is the most trustworthy thing in the world.

4.   A.   There are conflicts within an individual and between individuals because each individual has its own spirits. Thus, there is the existence of the spiritual conflict of individuality.

B. There are conflicts of tribes or races, because each tribe or race has its own spirits. Thus, there is the existence of tribal and racial spiritual conflicts.

C. The existence of spiritual conflicts has been an obstacle to worldly unification, or at least, being reasonable and peaceful.

D. Individual spirits, tribal spirits and racial spirits are too minor and unimportant to be a good reason for conflict. Thus, each person's spirits, tribal spirits and racial spirits can move to a higher level by looking at our common humanity rather than the separation of color, culture or religion. Those separating tendencies have limited meaning for any individual who lives in the stage of post-Heaven. This means when a natural spirit enters birth in a certain place, society and race, although separating tendencies are there, they are not ultimately important. In the pre-Heaven stage, which is before one obtains the form of life, there is no existence of any such barriers among all souls.

5.   Become open to the universal spiritual nature to dissolve individual, tribal and racial spirits into the universal spirits. This is a great exchange of what is temporal for what is eternal, what is low for the highest, small for the enormous, and what is shallow for the most profound.

6. Trust that the universe is one life being. Trust that the entire human race is one person. Trust that all religions are a partial description of the universal spiritual nature.

7. Trust God who is masculine and also feminine. God is always moving toward a positive result. Trust the removal of personal, tribal and racial negativity. God can be reached by the individual, tribe and race.

8. Progress of an individual or society must be broad and universal. Benefit to an individual or society must be broad and universal. This is moving toward God. Otherwise, narrowness and selfishness is moving toward the devil, which the ancients termed the negative and disharmonious trend of the individual, tribe or race.

9. All customs are the language that a local community and a society speak. Spiritual reality or God is universal language.
   The *Tao Teh Ching* describes the spiritual maturity that the human race reached some time ago. The *I Ching* expresses the exploration of the universal subtle law, and *Chuang Tzu* carries the voice of the freedom of life. These works were corrected from the old versions traditionally called the Three Scriptures of Mysticism. These three books are the center of the teaching of this tradition, which is specifically termed the Integral Way. A good teaching does not follow the conventional steps of establishing its own tradition and rejecting the others, but it aims at dissolving the conflict among all individuality, tribes and races to unite spiritually as the universal immortal being.

10. Tao or the subtle origin is the spiritual unity of the human race. When you want to learn spiritual reality, it means that you are ready to accept the better, higher and more truthful discoveries which the ancient achieved ones also discovered.

11. Specific spiritual practices of traditional nature and the value of truth are given in different teaching occasions. These can be separately learned as practical spiritual support and cultivation.

X. Reaching Spiritual Clarity and Purity Is How to Attain Your Spiritual Health
Most people are not aware that there are levels to spiritual learning. Strange, false, mixed-up, and something that deals

with voodoo or disembodied spirits describe the content of general, unachieved Taoism. Those words do not describe the teaching of the true tradition of genuine spirituality.

Once someone asked a famous painter what was the easiest thing to paint. His response was, "A ghost." People asked him why, to which he replied, "Because nobody has seen one." Nobody can prove exactly what a ghost looks like, thus the painter cannot be judged or determined to be right or wrong. I am using this example to describe that on the level of human communication, people cannot judge something that they do not know anything about. Some religious teachers or some teachers of Chi Kung (Chi Gong) thus can play on people's psychology by talking about strange things people have never heard about, such as powers which nobody can really exhibit. Their twisted way of talking makes people marvel, although it is absurdity; however, they still trust that it is the truth. Many false teachers say that they channel spirits. Those spirits are most often literary creations produced from the mouth and imagination of false teachers. Among these teachers and practitioners of face reading, geomancy, etc., perhaps 1 in 10,000 is honest and truthful. All this type of knowledge needs to be filtered and reorganized in order to continue the effective service.

I do not wish to be responsible for preconditioning you to trust teaching that people call "Taoist teaching" and then have you fall prey to their misleading schemes. I wish to warn you to study objectively and learn how to apply your own judgment. In that way, you can move to higher levels without being fooled. If you do not understand or know about something, do not believe it or trust it. Learn more about it from reading, or just work at the level where you are now. When you yourself move one step higher, then you can decide whether or not what somebody has said is true. Although you study, your understanding still depends upon your spiritual discernment. Your level of growth determines what is the most truthful, useful and helpful teaching for you at that particular time.

Some teachers minimize unnecessary personal contact with students and friends in order to avoid the inevitable misunder-standing which occurs when people of different stages of growth come together. To live independently is the lifestyle of the traditional, most truly achieved one who really does not wish to be recognized as a teacher.

Human people are energy. Energy has different levels. Even the one energy within a single individual manifests or is seen at different levels at different times. To cultivate oneself spiritually is to refine the lower quality energy to be high quality energy. However, truthful achievement occurs still higher above this foundation. When you experience the different, higher energy by contacting a teacher, please do not trust that you have received all the truth. A momentary experience is far away from truth or is only a limited experience of truth. The basic practice is to confirm yourself as a good human being. This is an ongoing event. A person who does so never has evil intention or the desire to harm someone else, because this person knows that harmful intent really harms one's own spiritual quality.

Never trust or respect people who talk to you and tell you marvelous things which they can use to promote their own excessive gain. I am not talking about fair exchange, I am talking about unfair exchange. I came from a society which had many such individuals. I know what people do that can harm others. Such things still occur in contemporary Chinese society. In China, Taoism on the level of the masses has changed to become a kind of spiritual cultural pollution, including so-called Chi Kung, spiritual healing, channelling, hocus pocus, etc. This is why the truly achieved ones almost always lived in the mountains or were hermits within their society.

So-called Chi Kung is associated with the low level of your energy. It is the more physical level. I am not talking about Chi Kung exercise such as taught by many people. I am talking about some type of Chi Kung declared to have a great deal of power. Your energy can be stirred up by suggestions. A suggestion can be made verbally or by the posture of body, hand, fingers, etc. They key point of hypnosis is to use suggestion. Hypnosis is not Tao and not spiritual truth.

People are made of energy. It depends on themselves whether they sublimate the crude foundation to be high essence. Before anybody achieves spiritual mastery within oneself, it is possible to accept a suggestion or hint to move in a direction in which some evil people wish to conduct you. Once you accept the hint or agree with them, then you lose your senses. One example is religious martyrs and the people who die in wars for the leaders' extreme reasons. They are managed and controlled by thoughts or ideas which they accept as truth, but which practically are not. This is why true spiritual achievement is so important. It is to support yourself without being a victim of somebody's suggestion or program.

Tao, or natural spiritual truth, is doing nothing of any kind. The Integral Way can be defined as the process or proceeding to move from the lower level to develop higher. Unfortunately, some ordinary Chi Kung teachers or religious promoters only play with the lower level and never take the students higher. This does not help yourself or themselves. Their knowledge of this level is enough to create a condition in which people feel they are being helped, without any real progress being made.

Spiritual achievement is internal. Clarity of mind and purity of spirit are developed from the unrefined coarseness of general life being.

In my books, I have described some marvelous things which are beyond your experience. They are what I learned and I proved to myself not merely something I have heard about. Also, I am still on the way to further learning. I mention these interesting things to promote your own growth or inspire you to seek the reality of what they are. Some religious or Chi Kung teachers in China use similar marvelous stories to support their manipulation of other people. They only talk about achievements which they can never reach to make people trust them.

How do you distinguish who is telling the truth? You cannot answer. You cannot tell by the way a teacher describes things. If it is a matter of personal experience of a teacher, then it has some validity. I suggest that my students and readers observe the motivations of those who relate marvelous tales of human events.

The true, traditional spirit of learning the Integral Way is that you can make friends with Lao Tzu, Chuang Tzu or any achieved one who lived thousands of years ago. They can help your growth when you read their books. There is no need for direct physical contact with a teacher.

Before they obtain spiritual development, individuals or a society can be lead by others in either a good or bad direction. Only the spiritually developed ones have clear vision or direction, but they cannot be relied upon to tackle the problems of the world without the understanding of all people.   When the majority of people are developed, then people of evil intention or who are just undeveloped will no longer be able to conduct or guide society in a destructive direction.

Chapter Conclusion

The ancestral achieved ones developed the deep knowledge of nature and of the life nature of human beings. They also knew the truthful connection between the two. Because all lives are truly connected with nature, if we extend ourselves in a partial direction by establishing preference, prejudice, hostility, ideology or discrimination, it is our own fault. Partial extension means spiritual self-diminishment.   Yet, all of these things developed further after organized religion began. Thus, partiality, preference, prejudice, etc., became the essential ingredients of ordinary organized religions. Although true spiritual leaders such as Lao Tzu and others before and after him did not extend themselves in a partial direction, when ordinary religions were developed, partiality, prejudice, etc. occurred.

I continue the truthful spiritual practice, which is above any ideological bondage or religious customs. Some religious leaders feel uneasy because I never express support for what they do. As I see it, what I continue is the universal religious spirit rather than any social custom or establishment. Social establishments and customs are barriers or walls which prevent people from seeing the universal spiritual unity which exists among all people. We can put our focus upon China as an example of the development of ordinary religions which do not serve universal spiritual unity. Folk Taoism, for example, is one of the social establishments and customs which has become a barrier to unity. I see the disbenefit and confusion that any single religion with its limitations can cause, and I believe it is not worth continuing this sort of teaching.

Folk Taoism is an example of how religion can confuse people. Life itself contains all types of desires. This is normal, but undeveloped people use religion to fulfill their disguised desires. By disguised desires I mean subconscious desires for money, power, social status and influence, etc. It is an inescapable reality that people develop and utilize religion as one type of culture to suppress those desires but yet fulfill them by disguised means. In other words, people form and develop religions or use existing religions to provide an excuse for unachieved desire. They develop entire cultures around their subconscious desires, finding fulfillment in conceptually contorted ways. Here, I am talking specifically about people who follow religions and people who lead different branches of folk Taoism. You can find evidence of this in their lives. This type of thing is not limited to folk Taoism.

Most religion includes insistence upon prejudice and hostility for racial or ideological reasons. An example of this is when religions fight "holy wars." Prejudice and hostility can all be ignored by truthful spiritual students and teachers. It is my hope that all of us follow a correct spiritual direction instead. A correct spiritual direction of a person or a nation is not different from a balanced life which extends itself reasonably, with consideration for the peace, health and growth of all. With a correct spiritual direction, each person or nation unselfishly helps other people further their development.

Each natural person has spiritual energy. If a person with spiritual energy is undeveloped, that energy can be misapplied in a destructive and evil direction. Only when one's personal physical spirits attain harmony with the high spirits can the narrow vision of the personal spirits become a broad, higher vision which encompasses all people and all lives. Only then is a healthy spiritual condition present. When healthy spiritual beings are present, then all possible benefit can be brought to an individual life. Then, all things and beings which surround you will work together with you for a positive purpose.

The correct, balanced purpose of religious worship is not to ask God to do something for you. I cannot accept any promotion that leads people in this direction. This type of religious understanding is an attempt to bend God to fulfill one's own personal interest. Its opposite extreme is the practice of religious martyrdom, or negative and meaningless sacrifice for narrow spiritual purpose, which is also not correct. The correct way to use a religion is to use its form to develop your own spiritual innocence, piety and purity. In doing so, you can attain personal spiritual development. Spiritual development means bringing clarity to the mind and subtle light to the spirit. This is the correct goal of religious and spiritual practice.

In other words, the real goal of religious practice is not to make God help you have more money and power, or to become more noble or prosperous. Doubtless these are not bad things, however, unless they are used incorrectly by people. Conventional religions condemn and disrespect them, but they still need them and rely on them.

A universal, truthful religious practice establishes personal spiritual development as the main goal of life. That development can allow you to have more money, influence and respect as a side product, but those things are not the goal. Again, I repeat, the goal is to bring clarity to the mind and subtle light to the spirit. If you understand that, you are my spiritual friend. That is the true direction of spiritual work. I encourage people to seek this, not only in later years, but especially when they are young and in the mainstream of life. It is important to remember that your focus in life is spiritual learning for spiritual development. Those who have no such focus experience that their life has no direction.

It is ancient custom in many places to set up festivals, and in those festivals to encourage people to make offerings. This was done in old China 40 years ago, in India now, and in many other places as well. Most conventional societies have a yearly big gathering with a major offering, and smaller seasonal or monthly offerings. Celebrations, festivals and offerings are still one of the main parts of their lives. Making an offering symbolizes the individual's personal concern for spiritual mastery of one's own life being. Making an offering is one simple universal spiritual practice. In Christianity, people pray before eating. In Catholicism, they celebrate mass. These are both types of offering. Any person, who before eating sits for a quiet moment or with both hands holds the main dish toward the sky, is making an offering. What is it that is being offered? Surely not the food, because you eat it afterward. What is being offered when a person goes to mass? The offering is your upright personality and healthy discipline. You offer your sincerity, uprightness and correctness so that the world may not be polluted by your presence or activities.

The most practical spiritual practice is offering one's heart for the common benefit. Giving one's heart does not mean insisting upon one's personal interest or opinions. This is the most fundamental offering.

Some religious Taoists are unhappy about my straightforward talk about their spiritual rituals and practices, which are merely symptomatic of unachieved expectations. They do not see what needs to be brought to the world by their lives. This type of psychological practice only expresses the introverted tendency, not the healthy spiritual direction of human multi-culture. From my own personal reflection upon what religious practices really mean, I have been working to offer my life and all my achievement to the universal unity of Tao, the subtle origin. Tao is the subtle center of gravity when we move along and enjoy the gift of the multi-culture and multi-religions.

When we talk about the totality of spiritual energy, internal and external, individual and public, all of what we talk about is spiritual truth. When we refer to the spiritual energy of the head, we call it God. God is part of Tao, the subtle origin. The subtle origin is all gods and the totality of the organic life force of the universe.

The old religion of one God was the attempt of social leaders who wished to establish their religion as a conquering force in denial of all others. Monotheistic religions in the past used the concept of one God to establish social control through uniformity. Their use of uniformity is echoed by the use of uniformity in communistic pursuits later. Neither the old religions nor the communists allow the existence of differences.

On a higher level, religions which believe in one God and those which believe in many gods all express variety in universal creativeness. The achievement of a developed one is finding unity in variety; this is where the teaching of the Integral Way develops. Conventional, dominant monotheism by itself does not fit the tendency of a natural life and the life trends toward democracy, which is closer to natural principles of government.

Life is a religion. Religious structures lose their foundation when they are built aside from the real practice of life. The spirit of variety assists individual progress to find the best expression in life and best utility of things from the ingenuity of the mind.

The old one-God, dominant religion went against nature by

attempting to establish a controlling force. The old-style religions expressed the spiritual defect of human life. They did not follow the naturalness of human life. Finding agreement or unity within variety is to find natural spiritual truth. Spiritual reality allows the existence of difference, but reaches the essence behind the differences.

The truthful guidance above all religions, whether one God or all gods, serves the spiritual development of all people in all generations. Yet all religions, whether one God or all gods, contain the following guidance:

When one's destiny and heart are good,
*   one will enjoy a good life.*
If one's heart and soul are good, but destiny is not good,
*   one will still receive protection from the subtle realm.*
If one's destiny is good, but the heart is bad
*   and the soul is falling,*
*   one will be finished soon.*
If one's destiny, heart and soul are bad,
*   one will suffer from all troubles.*

Destiny is the form of one's external
*   and internal environment,*
*   the soul is the center.*
Destiny affects only the shell as the surface of life.
Destiny is what the physical body and the emotion rely upon.
However, destiny is no destiny.
Destiny changes.
The soul which resides in life experiences all
*   as the process of refinement and higher evolution.*

One who gives oneself to the influence of destiny,
*   but does not cultivate one's heart and soul,*
*   shall have a fruitless life.*
One who keeps rectifying one's heart and soul
*   from falling to the bottomless pit of destruction*
*   will build one's deep root of eternal life.*

Is this not the universal religion that all people need to keep in mind?

Conclusion

I have given two versions of the life of Master Chen Tuan. It would seem appropriate to let my readers develop their own discernment about his life. I would only like to add that for Master Chen Tuan, the first version contains more elements of fact than elements of literature. I would now like to discuss one point in his story, when Emperor Sung Tai Tsung asked Master Chen Tuan for advice in selecting his third son to be heir to the throne. Master Chen Tuan gave his advice in a way that was practical and wise, because the emperor had basically already decided to choose the third son. This does not mean that Master Chen Tuan did not read the energy of people or that he did not have good judgment. I am just making the point that in a general situation as advisor, it is difficult for a person to say anything different when a thing is already decided. Any wise advisor needs to be sensitive to this.

I would like to share with you my personal experience when people come to me asking for advice through a birth chart reading or *I Ching* consultation. Many times young couples come to ask me whether they should be married, or the woman of a couple who is already pregnant asks me whether she should have an abortion. For the most part, these individuals have already made their decision and just want to confirm it. Thus, I cannot say too much.

Let us come to the subject of choosing an emperor. I feel it is important to understand something about leaders and leadership. Thus I would like to use the example of a group of wild horses. There is always one male horse who serves as the leader of the group of females. The way the lead horse moves into the position of leadership is a combination of internal and external choice. In other words, the horse did not make the decision entirely by itself; it was a joint decision made by the horse's constitution and the situation. The selection process of leaders happens through competition and fighting to see who is the strongest. There is lots of biting and kicking. Also, the ability to run fastest and lead all other horses is an important point. On the part of the winner, it is his self-effort, strength and good natural constitution that makes the difference. On the part of the other males, it is the result of winning the competition. Thus, generally, the strongest male becomes the leader.

In human society, through over 4,000 years of written history, the later emperors of Chinese society came to power in a similar way as the horses did. You could call this natural selection. The ironic thing about this aspect of Chinese history is that after great fighting and competition, these emperors still considered themselves to be the "Sons of Heaven." Son of Heaven was the title of respect given to ancient leaders who gave assistance to people after having been given power by them because of their natural and peaceful ways.

Some old teachings state that their people are the chosen people of God. It is a positive thought. Being God-chosen might be one supportive reason for a race to survive. Yet, if people do not make self-effort for survival, I do not think their tribe will be the only survivor, because God loves all people. In daily life, there must be an open vision for all races, tribes and individuals in the struggle for survival.

Spiritually, it is self-recognition as the one chosen by God. Each person must make an effort to achieve himself or herself in the right area. This is true of anyone whether a spiritual leader, monarch, ordinary person, or anyone else.

Truthfully, there is no competition whatsoever in spiritual achievement. This is because true spiritual achievement is a totally internal attainment; it cannot even be seen by others. However, once you express your internal attainment to the world, the rules of the game change; now you follow different laws. You run into competition. Is there any special spiritual support given to an achieved person? No, but there is a good maxim to follow. It is, "Do what you can do, and do not expect any return." Anyone who works in the world in any field will experience trouble.

So even for those who achieve themselves and decide to become spiritual teachers or leaders, the selection process is still similar to that of the lead horse. Your choice is not totally self-selection; it is also the choice of society. It is the choice of the stage of individual people's growth and the choice of the overall society at a given time in history. Once a person begins to teach, and understands the limitations of public acceptance, he can then decide how widely or deeply to teach.

The two masters, Master Kou Hong and Master Chen Tuan, share the spiritual source of my spiritual and family teachings. It is the true spirit of the teaching of the Integral Way aside from what some leaders in later times made into the mixed Taoist religion.

After Master Kou Hong ascended, his nephew edited some spiritual practices from Kou Hong's collection and made them into a book to develop the school of Ling Pao (Spiritual Treasure). He did this in order to adapt to his time, which was full of trouble, and people needed the support of spiritual practices other than enlightenment. Thus, this school did not include the enlightenment of Master Kou Hong.

In Master Kou Hong's collection, the main spiritual practices were called the Heritage of the Three Ages, the time of Heavenly Emperor, Earthly Emperor and Human Emperor. This refers to the collection of spiritual practices of the earliest people on earth. These practices were developed into the school of San Huang (Three Emperors). This school carried the teaching of mind, body and spirit. Practically that is what the three emperors metaphorically refer to. However, at the end of the Tang Dynasty (618-906 A.D.), which was the golden dynasty of Taoist development, the fires of war burned most of the books from this school. Thus, this school no longer existed after the Tang Dynasty. I learned some of the practices from this school through the teachers of my father. The practice from the Ling Pao school became one of the nine Taoist practices in later generations.

In the first version of Master Chen Tuan's life, there is a story about the five old men or five dragons. Please understand that they are spiritual practices, a metaphor which presents a hidden spiritual reality in Master Chen Tuan's cultivation. I include these practices in my teaching, too.

Master Chen Tuan, the influential spiritual person, lived in Wu Tan mountain. His T'ai Chi theory of human spirituality guided the development of T'ai Chi Ch'uan by Master Tsan, San Fong. Master Chen Tuan had three things to pass down: his achievement in the *I Ching* (I attained some of his achievement), his achievement in spiritual cultivation (I accept it and offer it as a foundation for understanding immortal practice) and his achievement in Dao-In, the 24 postures I adopted into my own Dao-In practice.[1]

Master Chen Tuan was born in Shih Chuang Province, so the spiritual hermits in Ching Chen mountain (Mountain Green City) also kept part of his heritage. He stayed in Hua Mountain after moving from Wu Tan mountain. Surely, the spiritual people of Hua mountain also carried the heritage of his teaching. Aside from initiating several traditions, he helped change the attitude of Confucianists from the pursuit of governmental position, fame and glory to the pursuit of the spiritual significance of life.

Yet what I have received from both of these masters is not something to be used in establishing a new tradition. What I have received from both masters is their spirit. Master Kou Hong's time was the time of magic. Spiritual teachers were only accepted if they did well at magic performance. The young Kou Hong had seen over 1,000 kinds of magic and miracle performances, but he concluded that they were not truly serviceable, they could only create a feeling of wonder. Basically, he concluded that magic performance was merely scatteredness, a waste of energy in serious spiritual pursuit. He said that this kind of power exposition could not be used to support the essence of life. Magic learning is not the right track of Taoist or spiritual learning, so Kou Hong was a truthful person. He was not attracted by magic, but he choose to embrace the simple essence himself. This is the wisdom of a great teacher. I have learned from Master Kou Hong, and his truthful attitude and responsible evolution. Although many practices in his book need explanation, his great heritage is his spirit.

Master Chen Tuan was an all-surpassing being. He chose to live a pure and dustless life, which means a life of no lower worldly interest. In Chinese culture, all scholars looked for sharing the ruling power; this was the social fashion, the only way to glorify their family name and personal life. It was the great influence of Master Chen Tuan to turn over, at the

---

[1]For more information, please refer to the book, *Attune Your Body with Dao-In* and videotape, which has the same name.

beginning of the Sung Dynasty (960-1279 A.D.), this unspiritual inclination. He had a number of students; most of them were great scholars who did not pursue social honors or high official positions in the royal court like the other scholars. He taught his students to focus beyond worldly life to deeply reach the vastness and profundity of universal life. He helped many young scholars become enlightened to work on personal internal worth rather than external world pursuit.

Master Chen Tuan was like a type of dragon or a phoenix on a high or super level of beingness of life. His example of spiritual culture did not extend to the majority; thus no personal worship was created. But he fulfilled his moral intention to subtly help the new strength of peace - the Sung Dynasty. He was not intending to give personal religious influence, either by religious worship or by promotion of any type of shallow Chi Kung (Chi Gong) practice. His long sleep, a sort of life hibernation, is the highest form of Chi Kung. Through his sleep, he achieved himself to give worldly service and also to have personal enjoyment. This means that while his physical body was asleep, another physical shape was somewhere else. If anybody degrades his name to promote any physical or emotional level practice, I think it is out of line, because such practice is achieved by incapacitating the physical body to work on the level of transportable energy. He could bi-locate his spirit to appear in different places to give service. Nobody, especially spiritual people, should use Chen Tuan's name to support any individual immature creation of different direction.

In this decade, I heard some people claim to give teachings under the name of Hua Shan School with the purpose of being related with Master Chen Tuan. In truth, such a school cannot have anything to do with Master Chen Tuan, because even the religious Taoist priests who lived on Hua Shan since the Yuan Dynasty do not have anything to do with Chen Tuan either. Those Taoist priests are related to the northern sect of religious Taoism, the Chuan Tse religion like the religious Taoism elsewhere. They have no connection with Master Chen Tuan, but they can declare they are of Hua San School by living there. What they practice is a Buddhist type of religion. It adds no glory to Master Chen's great sagely character.

Some people who carry the same surname as Chen claim to be Master Chen Tuan's blood descendants. It is totally unlikely, because Master Chen Tuan was an orphan, and he never married or raised a family. Master Chen Tuan was adopted into the Chen family by a fisherman, but Chen is not his real surname. It is Chinese craziness to look for an ancestor and erect the person as the family image. If it is truthful, the ancestors who made any good contribution should be respected.

There are several Chi Kung (Chi Gong) systems which may have value for physical benefit as exercise or whatever, but teachers who say that Master Chen Tuan practiced and transmitted it to them are not truthful. It is not straightforward. In the mixed Taoist practice, referring to a big name immortal as the initiator of a teaching or a program has been a custom in folk promotion. That was how religious Taoism was established.

From ancient times to the Tang Dynasty, the Chinese government did not make Taoism as a religious type of social promotion except the northern tribal government of North Wei (386-532 A.D.). The government accepted it mostly as personal spiritual learning and practice, with Lao Tzu's teaching carrying the spiritual direction. Surely, Tao as this ancient spiritual attainment is universally recognized. Lao Tzu received official decoration and was highly titled by the Tang Dynasty. The true reason for this acknowledgement is that the royal family's surname was Lee, which is also Lao Tzu's family name. The honor was given to Lao Tzu only, which had the side effect of indirectly increasing the social position of all the individual Taoist practitioners and mixed practitioners. Taoism as a religion was formally and officially sponsored by the government during the Sung Dynasty (960-1279 A.D.). Since that time, emperors were involved with religious establishment. The romantic and forceful emperor Hai Chung (1101-1126 A.D.) even declared himself the King of Tao. He mistakenly believed that religion could protect his kingdom.

Master Chen Tuan was one of the early type of natural personal spiritual cultivators who lived an absolutely individualized life. Although he had no social ambition, he was renowned among general people by his long sleep, which would last one hundred days or around three months. Surely it was a type of cultivation. To the world, his real cultural contribution was to reunite the Confucian school and Taoist school to become one again. He personally achieved spiritual excellence in the *I Ching*.

Some teachers declared that they received their practice from Chen Tuan. Practically, the source can hardly be validated, but they may truly have great respect and admiration for this great immortal. Master Chen Tuan was too high to be reachable by beginners, but these Chi Kung practices may serve as an appetizer for beginners. But it is untruthful to claim that Master Chen Tuan was achieved by doing those types of Chi Kung or that he himself created them for the world.

Master Chen Tuan's own practice was a personal expression of his immortal energy. Many other teachers created methods derived from what had been passed down by other ancient teachers of various development and reorganized them. Most of those teachers do not have knowledge to distinguish between the true way of genuine value and the incomplete practices created for the interest of the customers of general Chinese society. All those methods, properly promoted, are steps before reaching maturity.

Therefore, I offer this book to all of you, my readers who can absorb any good spiritual elements from Master Chen's example, to add to your personal nutrition for your deepest spiritual life. It is not my intention to support any one of the numerous Chi Kung schools, because Master Chen's spirit inspires us differently. Although we could not live a totally dustless life, there is no reason for us to take advantage of people when the dusty smog affects their spiritual vision.

What I have learned from Master Chen Tuan can be summarized by the following verse which was given by a third-generation scholar of his teaching who had the great inspiration to describe the spiritual mission of an achieved spiritual practitioner. It is:

Be the mind of Heaven and earth.
Be the life of all people.
Learn the spirit of the past sages.
Develop peace among the next ten thousand generations
    to come.

This is what guides me to maintain the original Taoist spirit, the spirit of the Divine Subtle Origin.

For society, the teachings of the Integral Way serve as public spiritual education. For individuals, the teachings guide internal spiritual practice. Therefore, the true teachings of the Integral Way cannot be mixed with any religions which use formality and damage the true independent spirit. Although some traditional practices have an external layout, which means design, arrangement or decorative display. The layout is only the symbol of the spiritual practice and postures which are for guiding or conducting energy in the body.

Since its beginning, this true tradition of spiritual teaching has been independent of social limitation. It has also never been involved in competition with any social religion. This tradition's goal is to help the spiritual development of individuals, the broad human society and all religion and culture. Its spiritual teaching is above the confusion of custom and fashionable thought which appear in the frame of time and location. The teaching of natural spiritual reality serves a sphere deeper and higher than the limited life of the body.

Poetry by Master Chen Tuan

When Chen Tuan lived in the mountain, he had a friend who learned from Master Lu, Tung Ping and who was called the Spiritual Person of Linen Clothes because of the plainness of his clothing. When Master Chen Tuan first left Hua Mountain, he wrote a short poem for him.

The way is divided at the foot of Hua Mountain.
Where we live, there are only a few grass huts
and a stream full of clouds.
You practice deafness to the worldly affairs and
the rights and wrongs of people.
This is how you maintain your virtue,
complete and long life.

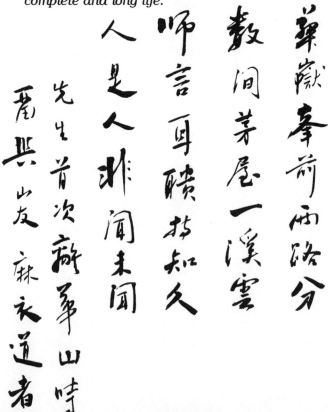

This is the poem given by Master of Linen Clothes as a response to Master Chen Tuan.

Singly I sit in the grass hut,
  far away from the glamour of the world.
I do not need the garment and the sacred bowl
  to life a life of the Zen monks in traveling.
I only know one thing:
  I do not talk about worldly things
  when I meet people.
This is how people leave me alone
  and I can be above the world's travails.

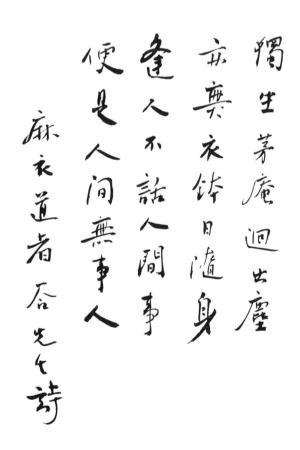

When Master Chen Tuan stayed in the capital, many people came to see him for advice because he was a great prophet. At that time, one scholar requested his teaching. This was his reply:

Once you take advantage of something,
*   never go again.*
Where you enjoy the most,
*   do not stay too long.*
If what you do and are
*   makes you feel you are great,*
Do not be there or do that again.

Note: Master Sou Yang praised this by saying: Valuable teaching given to us by a highly achieved person. One needs to learn that when one takes advantage of someone, it is one's own loss.

得便宜事，不可再去。
優游之所，勿可久戀。
得志之所勿再為。
先生應一士人請益贈語。
聞者以為至言。康節頌曰：
珍重至人留好語，
得便宜是隋便宜

The emperor wished to make Chen Tuan an advisor to the royal court, but he could not be kept in the capital. The high positions and the beautiful women offered to him did not have the kind of power to make him stay there. This is how he bid farewell to the emperor:

The high place in Hua Mountain
*   is my place.*
Anytime I am out of the house,
I am in the sky and riding on the wind.
I do not need any lock to lock my door.
It is always sealed by white clouds.

He hinted to the emperor that he did not need soldiers to protect his safety and the throne.

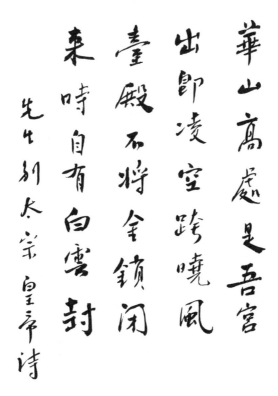

Here are two more poems by Master Chen Tuan:

Learning the Way enables you
to become pure and become quiet.
From being pure and quiet,
you learn to calm your spirits.
No greed and no attachment should be
allowed in your life flow.
Do not learn to be mean
from the world's fools.

The moon is my lamp.
Water is my mirror.
I take life support
from the long necked gourd.
I do not need people to support me,
whether I am out or in.
The golden turtle on the left,
and the white crane on the right,
guide my way.

Note: gourd means the body, golden turtle means the sunlight and white crane means the moonlight.

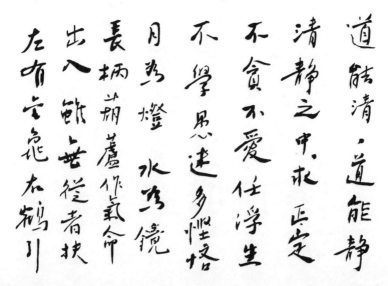

About Master Ni

The author, Master Ni, says he is lucky; everywhere he goes, he gives lectures without speaking very good English and yet people listen and understand. Perhaps 10% of the communication is by understanding his words; the rest is his personal sincerity and energy. However, he feels that it is his responsibility to ensure that people receive his message clearly and correctly, thus, he puts the lectures and classes in book form.

It is his great happiness to see the genuine progress of all people, all societies and nations as one big harmonized worldly community. This is the goal that makes him stand up to talk and write as one way of fulfilling his personal duty.

What he offers people comes from his own growth and attainment. He began his personal spiritual pursuit when he was ten years old. Although his spiritual nature is innate, expressing it suitably and usefully requires world experience and learning.

When he is asked to give personal information, he says that there is personally nothing useful or worthy of mention. He feels that, as an individual, he is just one of all people living on the same plane of life and therefore he is not special. A hard life and hard work has made him deeper and stronger, or perhaps wiser. This is the case with all people who do not yield to the negative influences of life and the world.

He likes to be considered a friend rather than be formally titled because he enjoys the natural spiritual response between himself and others who come together to extend the ageless natural spiritual truth to all.

He has been a great traveller. He has been in many places, and he never tires of going to new places. His books have been printed in different languages as a side offering to his professional work as a natural healer - a fully trained Traditional Chinese Medical doctor. He understands that his world mission is to awaken many people, and his friends and helpers conjointly fulfill the world spiritual mission of this time.

BOOKS IN ENGLISH BY MASTER NI

The Time is Now for a Better Life and a Better World - *New Publication*
What is the purpose of achievement? Is it just self-preservation or is it to exercise whatever you have attained from your spiritual cultivation to serve the public by improving the life of the majority of people? Master Ni offers his profound vision of our modern day spiritual dilemma to help us awaken to combine our personal necessity with the better survival of universal society. 136 pages, Softcover, Stock No. BTIME, $10.95

The Way, the Truth and the Light - *New Publication!*
Of all teachings by famous worldly sages, the teaching of this highly exalted sage in this book expresses the Way closest to that of Lao Tzu. The genuine life of this young sage links the spiritual achievement of east and west which highlights the subtle truth.   232 pages, Softcover, Stock No. BLIGH, $14.95

Life and Teaching of Two Immortals, Volume 2: Chen Tuan - *New Publication!*
The second emperor of the Sung Dynasty entitled Master Chen Tuan "Master of Subtle Reality." Master Ni describes his life and cultivation and gives in-depth commentaries which provide teaching and insight into the achievement of this highly respected Master. 192 pages, Softcover, Stock No. BLIF2, $12.95

Esoteric Tao Teh Ching - *New Publication!*
Tao Teh Ching has great profundity in philosophy and spiritual meaning, and can be understood in many ways and on many levels. In this new previously unreleased edition, Master Ni gives instruction for spiritual practices, which includes in-depth information and important techniques for spiritual benefit. 192 pages, Softcover, Stock No. BESOT, $12.95

Golden Message - A Guide to Spiritual Life with Self-Study Program for Learning the Integral Way - *New Publication!*
This volume begins with a traditional treatise by Master Ni's sons about the general nature of spiritual learning and its application for human life and behavior. It is followed by a message from Master Ni and an outline of the Spiritual Self-Study Program and Correspondence Course of the College of Tao. 160 pages, Softcover, Stock No. BGOLD, $11.95

Internal Alchemy: The Natural Way to Immortality - *New Publication!*
Ancient spiritually achieved ones used alchemical terminology metaphorically for human internal energy transformation. Internal alchemy intends for an individual to transform one's emotion and lower energy to be higher energy and to find the unity of life in order to reach the divine immortality. 288 pages, Softcover, Stock No. BALCH, $15.95

Mysticism: Empowering the Spirit Within - *New Publication!*
For more than 8,000 years, mystical knowledge has been passed down by sages. Master Ni introduces spiritual knowledge of the developed ones which does not use the senses or machines like scientific knowledge, yet can know both the entirety of the universe and the spirits. 200 pages, Softcover, Stock No. BMYST2, $13.95

Life and Teaching of Two Immortals, Volume 1: Kou Hong - *New Publication!*
Master Kou Hong was an achieved Master, a healer in Traditional Chinese Medicine and a specialist in the art of refining medicines who was born in 363 A.D. He laid the foundation of later cultural development in China. 176 pages, Softcover, Stock No. BLIF1, $12.95.

Ageless Counsel for Modern Life - *New Publication!*
These sixty-four writings, originally illustrative commentaries on the *I Ching*, are meaningful and useful spiritual guidance on various topics to enrich your life. Master Ni's delightful poetry and some teachings of esoteric Taoism can be found here as well. 256 pages, Softcover, Stock No. BAGEL, $15.95.

The Mystical Universal Mother
An understanding of both masculine and feminine energies are crucial to understanding oneself, in particular for people moving to higher spiritual evolution. Master Ni focuses upon the feminine through the examples of some ancient and modern women. 240 pages, Softcover, Stock No. BMYST, $14.95

Moonlight in the Dark Night
To attain inner clarity and freedom of the soul, you have to control your emotions. This book contains wisdom on balancing the emotions, including balancing love relationships, so that spiritual achievement becomes possible. 168 pages, Softcover, Stock No. BMOON, $12.95

Harmony - The Art of Life
Harmony occurs when two different things find the point at which they can link together. Master Ni shares valuable spiritual understanding and insight about the ability to bring harmony within one's own self, one's relationships and the world. 208 pages, Softcover, Stock No. BHARM, $14.95

Attune Your Body with Dao-In
The ancients discovered that Dao-In exercises solved problems of stagnant energy, increased their health and lengthened their years. The exercises are also used as practical support for cultivation and higher achievements of spiritual immortality. 144 pages, Softcover with photographs, Stock No. BDAOI, $14.95 Also on VHS, Stock No. VDAOI, $39.95

The Key to Good Fortune: Refining Your Spirit
Straighten Your Way *(Tai Shan Kan Yin Pien)* and The Silent Way of Blessing *(Yin Chia Wen)* are the main guidance for a mature, healthy life. Spiritual improvement can be an integral part of realizing a Heavenly life on earth. 144 pages, Softcover, Stock No. BKEYT, $12.95

Eternal Light
Master Ni presents the life and teachings of his father, Grandmaster Ni, Yo San, who was a spiritually achieved person, healer and teacher, and a source of inspiration to Master Ni. Some deeper teachings and understandings on living a spiritual life and higher achievement are given. 208 pages, Softcover, Stock No. BETER, $14.95

Quest of Soul
Master Ni addresses many concepts about the soul such as saving the soul, improving the soul's quality, the free soul, what happens at death and the universal soul. He guides and

inspires the reader into deeper self-knowledge and to move forward to increase personal happiness and spiritual depth. 152 pages, Softcover, Stock No. BQUES, $11.95

Nurture Your Spirits
Master Ni breaks some spiritual prohibitions and presents the spiritual truth he has studied and proven. This truth may help you develop and nurture your own spirits which are the truthful internal foundation of your life being. 176 pages, Softcover, Stock No. BNURT, $12.95

Internal Growth through Tao
Master Ni teaches the more subtle, much deeper sphere of the reality of life that is above the shallow sphere of external achievement. He also clears the confusion caused by some spiritual teachings and guides you in the direction of developing spiritually by growing internally. 208 pages, Softcover, Stock No. BINTE, $13.95

Power of Natural Healing
Master Ni discusses the natural capability of self-healing, information and practices which can assist any treatment method and presents methods of cultivation which promote a healthy life, longevity and spiritual achievement. 230 pages, Softcover, Stock No. BHEAL, $14.95

Essence of Universal Spirituality
In this volume, as an open-minded learner and achieved teacher of universal spirituality, Master Ni examines and discusses all levels and topics of religious and spiritual teaching to help you understand the ultimate truth and enjoy the achievement of all religions without becoming confused by them. 304 pages, Softcover, Stock No. BESSE, $19.95

Guide to Inner Light
Drawing inspiration from the experience of the ancient achieved ones, modern people looking for the true source and meaning of life can find great teachings to direct and benefit them. The invaluable ancient development can teach us to reach the attainable spiritual truth and point the way to the Inner Light. 192 pages, Softcover, Stock No. BGUID, $12.95

Stepping Stones for Spiritual Success
In this volume, Master Ni has taken the best of the traditional teachings and put them into contemporary language to make them more relevant to our time, culture and lives. 160 pages, Softcover, Stock No. BSTEP, $12.95.

The Complete Works of Lao Tzu
The *Tao Teh Ching* is one of the most widely translated and cherished works of literature. Its timeless wisdom provides a bridge to the subtle spiritual truth and aids harmonious and peaceful living. Also included is the *Hua Hu Ching*, a later work of Lao Tzu which was lost to the general public for a thousand years. 212 pages, Softcover, Stock No. BCOMP, $12.95

The Book of Changes and the Unchanging Truth
The legendary classic *I Ching* is recognized as the first written book of wisdom. Leaders and sages throughout history have consulted it as a trusted advisor which reveals the appropriate action in any circumstance. Includes over 200 pages of background material on natural energy cycles, instruction and commentaries. 669 pages, Stock No. BBOOK, Hardcover, $35.00

The Story of Two Kingdoms
This volume is the metaphoric tale of the conflict between the Kingdoms of Light and Darkness. Through this unique story, Master Ni transmits esoteric teachings of Taoism which have been carefully guarded secrets for over 5,000 years. This book is for those who are serious in achieving high spiritual goals. 122 pages, Stock No. BSTOR, Hardcover, $14.50

The Way of Integral Life
This book includes practical and applicable suggestions for daily life, philosophical thought, esoteric insight and guidelines for those aspiring to serve the world. The ancient sages' achievement can assist the growth of your own wisdom and balanced, reasonable life. 320 pages, Softcover, Stock No. BWAYS, $14.00. Hardcover, Stock No. BWAYH, $20.00.

Enlightenment: Mother of Spiritual Independence
The inspiring story and teachings of Master Hui Neng, the father of Zen Buddhism and Sixth Patriarch of the Buddhist tradition, highlight this volume. Hui Neng was a person of ordinary birth, intellectually unsophisticated, who achieved himself to become a spiritual leader. 264 pages, Softcover, Stock No. BENLS, $12.50   Hardcover, Stock No. BENLH, $22.00.

Attaining Unlimited Life
Chuang Tzu was perhaps the greatest philosopher and master of Tao. He touches the organic nature of human life more deeply and directly than do other great teachers. This volume also includes questions by students and answers by Master Ni.   467 pages, Softcover, Stock No. BATTS $18.00; Hardcover, Stock No. BATTH, $25.00.

The Gentle Path of Spiritual Progress
This book offers a glimpse into the dialogues between a Master and his students. In a relaxed, open manner, Master Ni, Hua-Ching explains to his students the fundamental practices that are the keys to experiencing enlightenment in everyday life. 290 pages, Softcover, Stock No. BGENT, $12.95.

Spiritual Messages from a Buffalo Rider, A Man of Tao
Our buffalo nature rides on us, whereas an achieved person rides the buffalo. Master Ni gives much helpful knowledge to those who are interested in improving their lives and deepening their cultivation so they too can develop beyond their mundane beings. 242 pages, Softcover, Stock No. BSPIR, $12.95.

8,000 Years of Wisdom, Volume I and II
This two-volume set contains a wealth of practical, down-to-earth advice given by Master Ni over a five-year period. Drawing on his training in Traditional Chinese Medicine, Herbology and Acupuncture, Master Ni gives candid answers to questions on many topics. Volume I includes dietary guidance; 236 pages; Stock No. BWIS1 Volume II includes sex and pregnancy guidance; 241 pages; Stock No. BWIS2. Softcover, each volume $12.50

Awaken to the Great Path
Originally the first half of the *Uncharted Voyage Toward the Subtle Light*, this volume offers a clear and direct vision of the spiritual truth of life. It explains many of the subtle truths which are obvious to some but unapparent to others. The Great Path is not the unique teaching, but it can show the way to the integral spiritual truth in every useful level of life. 248 pages, Softcover, Stock No. BAWAK, $14.95

Ascend the Spiritual Mountain
Originally the second half of the *Uncharted Voyage Toward the Subtle Light*, this book offers further spiritual understanding with many invaluable practices which may help you integrate your spiritual self with your daily life. In deep truth, at different times and places, people still have only one teacher: the universal spiritual self itself. 216 pages, Softcover, Stock No. BASCE, $14.95

Footsteps of the Mystical Child
This book poses and answers such questions as: What is a soul? What is wisdom? What is spiritual evolution? to enable readers to open themselves to new realms of understanding and personal growth. Includes true examples about people's internal and external struggles on the path of self-development and spiritual evolution. 166 pages, Softcover, Stock No. BFOOT, $9.50

The Heavenly Way
A translation of the classic Tai Shan Kan Yin Pien (Straighten Your Way) and Yin Chia Wen (The Silent Way of Blessing). The treatises in this booklet are the main guidance for a mature and healthy life. This truth can teach the perpetual Heavenly Way by which one reconnects oneself with the divine nature. 41 pages, Softcover, Stock No. BHEAV, $2.50

Workbook for Spiritual Development
This material summarizes thousands of years of traditional teachings and little-known practices for spiritual development. There are sections on ancient invocations, natural celibacy and postures for energy channeling. Master Ni explains basic attitudes and knowledge that supports spiritual practice. 240 pages, Softcover, Stock No. BWORK, $14.95

Poster of Master Lu
Color poster of Master Lu, Tung Ping (shown on cover of workbook), for use with the workbook or in one's shrine. 16" x 22"; Stock No. PMLTP. $10.95

The Taoist Inner View of the Universe
Master Ni has given all the opportunity to know the vast achievement of the ancient unspoiled mind and its transpiercing vision. This book offers a glimpse of the inner world and immortal realm known to achieved ones and makes it understandable for students aspiring to a more complete life. 218 pages, Softcover, Stock No. BTAOI, $14.95

Tao, the Subtle Universal Law
Most people are unaware that their thoughts and behavior evoke responses from the invisible net of universal energy. To lead a good stable life is to be aware of the universal subtle law in every moment of our lives. This book presents practical methods that have been successfully used for centuries to accomplish this. 165 pages, Softcover, Stock No. TAOS, $7.50

MATERIALS ON NATURAL HEALTH, ARTS AND SCIENCES

BOOKS

101 Vegetarian Delights - *New Publication!* by Lily Chuang and Cathy McNease
A vegetarian diet is a gentle way of life with both physical and spiritual benefits. The Oriental tradition provides helpful methods to assure that a vegetarian diet is well-balanced and nourishing. This book provides a variety of clear and precise recipes ranging from everyday nutrition to exotic and delicious feasts. 176 pages, Softcover, Stock No. B101V, $12.95

The Tao of Nutrition by Maoshing Ni, Ph.D., with Cathy McNease, B.S., M.H. - This book offers both a healing and a disease prevention system through eating habits. This volume contains 3 major sections: theories of Chinese nutrition and philosophy; descriptions of 100 common foods with energetic properties and therapeutic actions; and nutritional remedies for common ailments. 214 pages, Softcover, Stock No. BNUTR, $14.50

Chinese Vegetarian Delights by Lily Chuang
An extraordinary collection of recipes based on principles of traditional Chinese nutrition. For those who require restricted diets or who choose an optimal diet, this cookbook is a rare treasure. Meat, sugar, diary products and fried foods are excluded. 104 pages, Softcover, Stock No. BCHIV, $7.50

Chinese Herbology Made Easy - by Maoshing Ni, Ph.D.
This text provides an overview of Oriental medical theory, in-depth descriptions of each herb category, over 300 black and white photographs, extensive tables of individual herbs for easy reference and an index of pharmaceutical and Pin-Yin names. This book gives a clear, efficient focus to Chinese herbology. 202 pages, Softcover, Stock No. BCHIH, 14.50

Crane Style Chi Gong Book - By Daoshing Ni, Ph.D.
Chi Gong is a set of meditative exercises developed thousands of years ago in China and now practiced for healing purposes. It combines breathing techniques, body movements and mental imagery to guide the smooth flow of energy throughout the body. It may be used with or without the videotape. 55 pages. Stock No. BCRAN. Spiral-bound, $10.95

VIDEO TAPES

Attune Your Body with Dao-In (VHS) - by Master Ni. Dao-In is a series of movements traditionally used for conducting physical energy. The ancients discovered that Dao-In exercise solves problems of stagnant energy, increases health and lengthens one's years, providing support for cultivation and higher achievements of spiritual immortality. Stock No. VDAOI, VHS $39.95

T'ai Chi Ch'uan: An Appreciation (VHS) - by Master Ni.
Master Ni, Hua-Ching presents three styles of T'ai Chi handed down to him through generations of highly developed masters. "Gentle Path," "Sky Journey" and "Infinite Expansion" are presented uninterrupted in this unique videotape, set to music for observation and appreciation. Stock No. VAPPR. VHS 30 minutes $24.95

Crane Style Chi Gong (VHS) - by Dr. Daoshing Ni, Ph.D.
Chi Gong is a set of meditative exercises practiced for healing chronic diseases, strengthening the body and spiritual enlightenment. Correct and persistent practice will increase one's energy, relieve tension, improve concentration, release emotional stress and restore general well-being. 2 hours, Stock No. VCRAN. $39.95

Eight Treasures (VHS) - By Maoshing Ni, Ph.D.
These exercises help open blocks in your energy flow and strengthen your vitality. It is a complete exercise combining physical stretching, toning and energy-conducting movements coordinated with breathing. Patterned from nature, its 32 movements are an excellent foundation for T'ai Chi Ch'uan or martial arts. 1 hour, 45 minutes. Stock No. VEIGH. $39.95

T'ai Chi Ch'uan I & II (VHS) - By Maoshing Ni, Ph.D.
This exercise integrates the flow of physical movement with that of internal energy in the Taoist style of "Harmony," similar to the long form of Yang-style T'ai Chi Ch'uan. Tai Chi has been practiced for thousands of years to help both physical longevity and spiritual cultivation. 1 hour each. Each video tape $39.95. Order both for $69.95. Stock Nos: Part I, VTAI1; Part II, VTAI2; Set of two, VTAI3.

AUDIO CASSETTES

Invocations for Health, Longevity and Healing a Broken Heart - By Maoshing Ni, Ph.D.
This audio cassette guides the listener through a series of ancient invocations to channel and conduct one's own healing energy and vital force. "Thinking is louder than thunder. The mystical power which creates all miracles is your sincere practice of this principle." 30 minutes, Stock No. AINVO, $9.95

Stress Release with Chi Gong - By Maoshing Ni, Ph.D.
This audio cassette guides you through simple, ancient breathing exercises that enable you to release day-to-day stress and tension that are such a common cause of illness today. 30 minutes. Stock No. ACHIS. $9.95

Pain Management with Chi Gong - By Maoshing Ni, Ph.D.
Using easy visualization and deep-breathing techniques developed over thousands of years, this audio cassette offers methods for overcoming pain by invigorating your energy flow and unblocking obstructions that cause pain. 30 minutes, Stock No. ACHIP. $9.95

Tao Teh Ching **Cassette Tapes**
This classic work of Lao Tzu has been recorded in this two-cassette set that is a companion to the book translated by Master Ni. Professionally recorded and read by Robert Rudelson. 120 minutes. Stock No. ATAOT. $12.95

Order Master Ni's book, *The Complete Works of Lao Tzu,* and *Tao Teh Ching* Cassette Tapes for only $23.00. Stock No. ABTAO.

This list is according to date of publication and Master Ni's own spiritual revelation, and offers a way to study his work.

1979:   *The Complete Works of Lao Tzu*
          The Taoist Inner View of the Universe
          Tao, the Subtle Universal Law
1983:   *The Book of Changes and the Unchanging Truth*
          8,000 Years of Wisdom, I
          8,000 Years of Wisdom, II
1984:   *Workbook for Spiritual Development*
1985:   *The Uncharted Voyage Toward the Subtle Light* (reprinted as
                 Awaken to the Great Path and
                 Ascend the Spiritual Mountain)
1986:   *Footsteps of the Mystical Child*
1987:   *The Gentle Path of Spiritual Progress*
          Spiritual Messages from a Buffalo Rider (originally
                 part of *Gentle Path of Spiritual Progress*)
1989:   *The Way of Integral Life*
          Enlightenment: Mother of Spiritual Independence
          Attaining Unlimited Life
          The Story of Two Kingdoms
1990:   *Stepping Stones for Spiritual Success*
          Guide to Inner Light
          Essence of Universal Spirituality
1991:   *Internal Growth through Tao*
          Nurture Your Spirits
          Quest of Soul
          Power of Natural Healing
          Eternal Light
          The Key to Good Fortune: Refining Your Spirit
1992:   *Attune Your Body with Dao-In*
          Harmony: The Art of Life
          Moonlight in the Dark Night
          Life and Teachings of Two Immortals, Volume I: Kou Hong
          The Mystical Universal Mother
          Ageless Counsel for Modern Times
          Mysticism: Empowering the Spirit Within
          The Time is Now for a Better Life and Better World
          Internal Alchemy: The Natural Way to Immortality
1993:   *Golden Message* (by Daoshing and Maoshing Ni, based on
                 the works of Master Ni, Hua-Ching)
          Esoteric Tao Teh Ching
          The Way, the Truth and the Light
          From Diversity to Unity: Spiritual Integration of the World
          Life and Teachings of Two Immortals, Volume II: Chen Tuan
          Immortal Wisdom
          By the Light of the North Star: Cultivating Your Spiritual Life
          Seeing the Unseen: The Reality of Universal Spiritual Beings

In addition, the forthcoming books will be compiled from his lecturing and teaching service:

Gentle Path T'ai Chi Ch'uan
Sky Journey T'ai Chi Ch'uan
Infinite Expansion T'ai Chi Ch'uan
Cosmic Tour Ba Gua Zahn
The Path of Constantly Developing Life

How To Order

Name: _____

Address: _____

City: _____ State: _____ Zip: _____

Phone - Daytime: _____ Evening: _____

(We may telephone you if we have questions about your order.)

Qty.	Stock No.	Title/Description	Price Each	Total Price

Total amount for items ordered_____

Sales tax (CA residents only, 8-1/4%)_____

Shipping Charge (see below)_____

Total Amount Enclosed_____

Visa _____ Mastercard _____ Expiration Date _____

Card number:_____

Signature:_____

Shipping: Please give full street address or nearest crossroads. If shipping to more than one address, use separate shipping charges. Please allow 2 - 4 weeks for US delivery and 6 - 10 weeks for foreign surface mail.

By Mail: Complete this form with payment (US funds only, No Foreign Postal Money Orders, please) and mail to: SevenStar Publications, 1314 Second St., Santa Monica, CA 90401

Phone Orders: You may leave credit card orders anytime on our answering machine. Please speak clearly and remember to leave your full name and daytime phone number. Call (800) 578-9526 to order or (310) 576-1901 for information..

Shipping Charges:

Domestic Surface: First item $3.25, each additional, add $.50.
Canada Surface: First item $3.25, each additional, add $1.00.
Canada Air: First item $4.00, each additional, add $2.00
Foreign Surface: First Item $3.50, each additional, add $2.00.
Foreign Air: First item $12.00, each additional, add $7.00.

All foreign orders: Add 5% of your book total to shipping charges to cover insurance.

_____ Please send me your complete catalog.

Thank you for your order

Spiritual Study and Teaching Through the College of Tao

A. Spiritual Learning

The College of Tao and the Union of Tao and Man were formally established in California in the 1970's, yet this tradition is a very old spiritual culture containing centuries of human spiritual growth. Its central goal is to offer healthy spiritual education to all people. This time-tested school values the spiritual development of each individual self and passes down its guidance and experience.

In carrying his heritage from its origin to the west, Master Ni chooses to avoid the mistake of old-style religions whose rigid practices ignore the delicacy of individual spiritual growth. He prefers to offer the teachings of his tradition as a school of no boundary to universal spiritual students.

Any interested individual is welcome to join and learn to grow for oneself. The Correspondence Course/Self-Study Program can be useful to you. The Program, which is based on Master Ni's books and videotapes, gives people who wish to study on their own or are too far from a center or volunteer teachers an opportunity to study the learning of the Way at their own speed. The outline of how to participate in the Correspondence Course/Self-Study Program can be found at the end of the book *The Golden Message*.

B. Spiritual Teaching in the United States and Abroad

New directives are adopted for the following reasons:

1. *To screen all teaching candidates and ensure the quality of all teaching of Master Ni's material and skills*
2. *To continue activity of this tradition in the modern world in the present time*
3. *To discourage improper usage or representation of Master Ni's teachings*
4. *To provide supervision of all teachers.*

Beginning January 1, 1993, anyone wishing to teach Master Ni's materials/techniques must affiliate with the College of Tao regardless of prior arrangement. A certificate will be given when an Affiliation Agreement is signed. The names and addresses of all affiliated teachers will be printed on a separate page and inserted in all book orders sent out from the College of Tao and SevenStar Communications.

If you are interested in affiliating with the Union of Tao and Man/College of Tao, please fill out the form below and mail it to the address indicated.

- -

Mail to: College of Tao, 1314 Second Street, Santa Monica, CA 90401

____ I wish to be put on the mailing list of the College of Tao and SevenStar Communications to be notified of classes, educational activities and new publications.

____ I am interested in the Correspondence Course/Self Study Program of the College of Tao. I have already read and understood the instruction for the Program printed in *The Golden Message*.

____ I am interested in becoming an affiliated teacher.

Name:_____

Address:_____

City:_____ State:_____ Zip:_____

Herbs Used by Ancient Taoist Masters

The pursuit of everlasting youth or immortality throughout human history is an innate human desire. Long ago, Chinese esoteric Taoists went to the high mountains to contemplate nature, strengthen their bodies, empower their minds and develop their spirit. From their studies and cultivation, they gave China alchemy and chemistry, herbology and acupuncture, the I Ching, astrology, martial arts and T'ai Chi Ch'uan, Chi Gong and many other useful kinds of knowledge.

Most important, they handed down in secrecy methods for attaining longevity and spiritual immortality. There were different levels of approach; one was to use a collection of food herb formulas that were only available to highly achieved Taoist masters. They used these food herbs to increase energy and heighten vitality. This treasured collection of herbal formulas remained within the Ni family for centuries.

Now, through Traditions of Tao, the Ni family makes these foods available for you to use to assist the foundation of your own positive development. It is only with a strong foundation that expected results are produced from diligent cultivation.

As a further benefit, in concert with the Taoist principle of self-sufficiency, Traditions of Tao offers the food herbs along with the Union of Tao and Man's publications in a distribution opportunity for anyone serious about financial independence.

Send to: Traditions of Tao
             1314 Second Street #208
             Santa Monica, CA 90401

Please send me a Traditions of Tao brochure.

Name _____

Address_____

City_____State_____Zip_____

Phone (day)_____(night)_____

Yo San University of Traditional Chinese Medicine

"Not just a medical career, but a life-time commitment to raising one's spiritual standard."

Thank you for your support and interest in our publications and services. It is by your patronage that we continue to offer you the practical knowledge and wisdom from this venerable Taoist tradition.

Because of your sustained interest in Taoism, in January 1989 we formed Yo San University of Traditional Chinese Medicine, a non-profit educational institution under the direction of founder Master Ni, Hua-Ching. Yo San University is the continuation of 38 generations of Ni family practitioners who handed down knowledge and wisdom from father to son. Its purpose is to train and graduate practitioners of the highest caliber in Traditional Chinese Medicine, which includes acupuncture, herbology and spiritual development.

We view Traditional Chinese Medicine as the application of spiritual development. Its foundation is the spiritual capability to know life, to diagnose a person's problem and how to cure it. We teach students how to care for themselves and other, emphasizing the integration of traditional knowledge and modern science. Yo San University offers a complete Master's degree program approved by the California State Department of Education that provides an excellent education in Traditional Chinese Medicine and meets all requirements for state licensure.

We invite you to inquire into our university for a creative and rewarding career as a holistic physician. Classes are also open to persons interested only in self-enrichment. For more information, please fill out the form below and send it to:

Yo San University
of Traditional Chinese Medicine
1314 Second Street
Santa Monica, CA 90401

☐ Please send me information on the Masters degree program in Traditional Chinese Medicine.

☐ Please send me information on health workshops and seminars.

☐ Please send me information on continuing education for acupuncturists and health professionals.

Name _____

Address _____

City_____ State_____ Zip_____

Phone(day)_____ (evening)_____

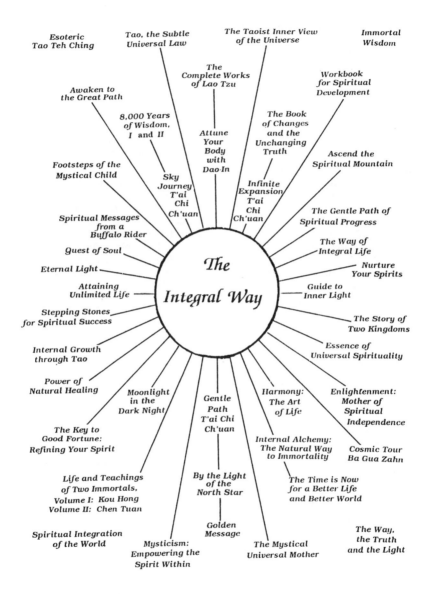

Esoteric
Tao Teh Ching

Tao, the Subtle
Universal Law

The Taoist Inner View
of the Universe

Immortal
Wisdom

The
Complete Works
of Lao Tzu

Workbook
for Spiritual
Development

Awaken to
the Great Path

8,000 Years
of Wisdom,
I and II

Attune
Your
Body
with
Dao-In

The Book
of Changes
and the
Unchanging
Truth

Ascend the
Spiritual Mountain

Footsteps of the
Mystical Child

Sky
Journey
T'ai
Chi
Ch'uan

Infinite
Expansion
T'ai
Chi
Ch'uan

The Gentle Path of
Spiritual Progress

Spiritual Messages
from a
Buffalo Rider

The Way of
Integral Life

Quest of Soul

Eternal Light

The

Integral Way

Nurture
Your Spirits

Attaining
Unlimited Life

Guide to
Inner Light

Stepping Stones
for Spiritual Success

The Story of
Two Kingdoms

Internal Growth
through Tao

Essence of
Universal Spirituality

Power of
Natural Healing

Moonlight
in the
Dark Night

Gentle
Path
T'ai Chi
Ch'uan

Harmony:
The Art
of Life

Enlightenment:
Mother of
Spiritual
Independence

The Key to
Good Fortune:
Refining Your Spirit

Internal Alchemy:
The Natural Way
to Immortality

Cosmic Tour
Ba Gua Zahn

Life and Teachings
of Two Immortals,
Volume I: Kou Hong
Volume II: Chen Tuan

By the Light
of the
North Star

The Time is Now
for a Better Life
and Better World

Spiritual Integration
of the World

Golden
Message

The Way,
the Truth
and the Light

Mysticism:
Empowering the
Spirit Within

The Mystical
Universal Mother

Index of Some Topics